"An amazing story of how City became a leading theologian and prophet of liberation theology in the Americas. Jorge's vision of uniting Catholics, Jews, and Protestants in solidarity with the poor and oppressed continues to inspire and unite people of faith. A great adventure story indeed!"
—John Fife, co-founder of the Sanctuary Movement for refugees from Central America

"How fortunate for me as a white, middle-class, privileged Texan to have found friendship and inspiration from Jorge Lara-Braud and his journey of interfaith inclusion. Jorge's solid grounding in his faith propelled him toward welcoming and embracing other spiritual paths, recognizing the richness and wholeness of God's love for all. He left this earthly world a better place and one more reflective of our interconnected humanity."
—Donna Howard, Texas State Representative; former board member, Interfaith Action of Central Texas

"*Dare to Adventure* tells how my dad's personal experiences ignited a passion to lead in resolving social injustices and helping to build bridges between people of different faiths and traditions. I felt every passage of this engaging real-life story was written particularly to me—for my knowledge, appreciation, and personal well-being. There is no one like my dad: a true believer and follower of Jesus's example of fighting for others and inspiring a mindset of Christian inclusiveness in the people he influenced."
—Jorge Luis Lara Marroquín, son of Jorge Lara-Braud, executive coach

Dare
to Adventure
LAS BIENAVENTURANZAS

Also by Gretchen Lara-Shartle

On Earth and In Heaven
Awakening Courage

Dare
to Adventure
LAS BIENAVENTURANZAS

The Life of Jorge Lara-Braud

Gretchen Lara-Shartle

Dare to Adventure, Las Bienaventuranzas:
The Life of Jorge Lara-Braud
© 2023, Gretchen Lara-Shartle. All rights reserved.

Published by Good Adventure Press, West Lake Hills, TX

ISBN: 978-1-7377956-3-6 (paperback)
ISBN: 978-1-7377956-4-3 (ebook)
Library of Congress Control Number: 2023911699

www.gretchenlarashartle.com

Scripture quotations indicated by (NRSV) are from the New Revised Standard Version Bible, copyright © 1989 by the National Council of Churches of Christ in the United States of America. Used by permission. All rights reserved worldwide.

Scripture quotations indicated by (IB) are from The Inclusive Bible: The First Egalitarian Translation, copyright © 2007 by Priests for Equality. Used by permission. All rights reserved worldwide.

All rights reserved. No part of this publication may be reproduced in any manner without written permission from the publisher except in the case of brief quotations embodied in critical articles and reviews.

For Jorge in Heaven

Isabella Knight, May 2022, isabellacknight.com

Remembrance stone for Jorge Lara-Braud in the "Placita de los Santos" at El Buen Pastor Church.

Contents

Foreword i
Preface vii
The Meaning of *Las Bienaventuranzas* and *Bienaventuranza* ix
Chapter One: Ugly Duckling 1
Chapter Two: A Season of Discovery 9
Chapter Three: From Paradise to the Barrio 15
Chapter Four: I Stand My Ground 27
Chapter Five: The Wellspring 33
Chapter Six: Moved to Boldness 43
Chapter Seven: My Dream 51
Chapter Eight: My Divided Heart 65
Chapter Nine: Opening People's Hearts 83
Chapter Ten: Anguish and Achievement 99
Chapter Eleven: Óscar Romero ¡Presente! 107
Chapter Twelve: Deeply Engaged 141
Chapter Thirteen: A Glimpse of Paradise 163
Chapter Fourteen: Can We Believe in God after This? 181
Chapter Fifteen: Springs in the Desert 207
Afterword 225
Acknowledgments 237
Appendix A 241
Appendix B 263
Notes 271
Bibliography 283

Foreword

On the Fourth of July 1980, as Americans celebrated our Declaration of Independence, a deputy sheriff and border patrol agents found three men lying in the brutal 120-degree heat of the Arizona desert. In a massive search over the next two days, they found twenty-seven more men and women, thirteen of whom had died from dehydration and heat stroke. These were Salvadorans who had crossed the border in Organ Pipe Cactus National Monument Wilderness hoping to get to Los Angeles. Instead they were lost and dying in a vast and unforgiving desert.

The survivors were brought to a hospital in Tucson, where I was one of several pastors who were called to help those who were traumatized by the agonizing deaths of their companions and their own suffering. Though familiar with the pastoral care of trauma victims, I was totally unprepared to deal with their stories about why they had fled El Salvador. They told me about family members murdered by death squads, friends being "disappeared" in the night, massacres of villages, and the fear and repression gripping the land.

I confess that I could not have located El Salvador on a map. I knew that it was somewhere between Mexico and Panama, but like many North Americans, I knew little or nothing about El Salvador, except that it was one of the "banana republics" of Central America. Obviously, I needed help to provide adequate pastoral care to the survivors in the hospital. I also wanted to help them avoid deportation back to El Salvador, the country they had fled to save their lives.

When I telephoned the mission office of the Presbyterian Church for advice, the staff person responded emphatically, "I could help you, but I think you had better call Dr. Jorge Lara-Braud. He was a close friend and adviser to Archbishop Óscar Romero from the National Council of Churches. He just testified before Congress about the situation in El Salvador."

Thus began my "good adventure" with Jorge Lara-Braud. When I called him, the voice on the phone sounded nothing like I expected. In impeccable English (with a slight Scottish lilt), Jorge responded to my story of the Salvadoran refugees with words I was to hear again and again over the years: "John, you need to understand . . ." And then, whatever the crisis or question I would bring to him, Jorge would begin with a clear understanding of the history, move to erudite analysis of the current situation in El Salvador, tell me the latest policy pronouncements of the State Department, teach me the details of counterinsurgency, or low-intensity warfare, from the Pentagon, and conclude with a brilliant theological analysis of the role of the church. This would all be summed up with a passionate personal story from Jorge's relationship with Archbishop Romero, or a verbatim quote.

Decades later, it is impossible to number these phone calls and meetings, but I shall always be grateful to God for the guidance and inspired education I received from Jorge. He became a mentor, professor, theological adviser, friend, and prophet to me through the decade of the 1980s. Whenever I called Jorge, whether he was serving at the National Council of Churches of the United States, or as director of the Council on Theology and Culture of the Presbyterian Church, or later as professor of theology at San Francisco Theological Seminary, he was always available to consult, counsel, and sometimes gently correct. The lengthy lectures that always began, "John, you need to understand . . . ," guided me through the decision to safely smuggle refugees across the border and to cofound the Sanctuary Movement in North America. This movement in the 1980s involved a long trial, three federal convictions, and finally a judicial victory that eventually led to new congressional laws on asylum. These laws allowed Central American refugees to seek sanctuary in the United States. Jorge Lara-Braud was telling the truth when he described the journey of faith as a "good adventure."

In this book, I pray you will discover some of the abundant gifts that Jorge lavished upon the whole church: countless students and colleagues, the ecumenical church, liberation theologians, congregations and conferences, Chicano organizations, and a struggling pastor in the borderlands. In his speech "1492–1992: Can We Believe in God after This?" (Appendix A of this book), Jorge focused on the 500 years of history since Columbus's arrival in this hemisphere. It is a clear and concise summary of that history and the complicity of the church in the conquest and genocide that followed.

Carefully researched and footnoted, this speech demonstrates the academic integrity of Jorge's work and leads the reader straight to the toughest theological question: "Can we believe in God after this?" Jorge's profound response is not apologetic, orthodox, nor an obscure reiteration of doctrine, but a head-on challenge to the idolatry of empire and conquest by the church of empire and conquest. He demands that a "distinction be made between the god of the abusers and the God of the abused."[1] Idols, as we know, are false gods. They have no power to do good, but they can do incalculable evil. Worse still, false gods demand human sacrifices: the poor, the sick, the young, the elderly, the immigrants, the unemployed, the strangers, the gays, the nonconformists, the unarmed. His conclusion is a call to redemption for all who suffer unjustly:

> Thank God this is a wounded God, not almighty in power, but almighty in love. And because love never dies, death will be conquered, resurrection will happen. It is happening now.[2]

That, he indicates, is the only good news that overcomes the bad news of the past and redeems history.

The contest for the future is fundamentally a contest that is spiritual and theological. It is on that spiritual battleground that the outcome of this contest will be determined in each of us and in history. What a daring adventure this invitation promises!

Journey with this immigrant from Mexico through his education in Catholic social teaching, the Protestant Reformation, the history of conquest and revolution, the promise of American ideals, guided by Jorge's unique ability to cross all of the traditional borders and stereotypes, to gain a new vision of God's liberating presence with the poor and oppressed in their struggle for justice.

Then the reader can join in the unfolding revelation of God's "preferential option for the poor."

My most cherished memories of Jorge center on his charismatic gift of storytelling, especially his stories of Archbishop Óscar Romero, the martyred saint of El Salvador. Here you will find stories not found anywhere else because they are unique to Jorge's personal relationship with the archbishop. You will also find classic stories of Romero's conversion to caring for the poor and oppressed of El Salvador and his plea to the soldiers to "stop the killing." What you must imagine is the passion and power with which Jorge could tell these stories of Romero, often with tears in his eyes.

In March 2002, a weeklong celebration of the Sanctuary Movement was held in Tucson. Pastors, rabbis, theologians, refugees, sanctuary volunteers, celebrities, and historians all gathered for a time of reflection and celebration. The culmination was worship on Sunday morning at Southside Church, where it all began. The only preacher who was up to that occasion was, of course, Jorge Lara-Braud. Parkinson's disease had taken a serious toll on Jorge by that time, but on that Sunday morning, the Spirit restored the passion to his preaching. To a packed church, overflowing to the sidewalks outside, Jorge told Archbishop Romero stories for almost an hour to a rapt congregation. But the sermon was not about the past; it was about the communion of the saints leading the church into God's "good adventure to you whose hearts are genuinely with the poor."[3]

As Jorge's journey and life and faith unfold in this book, our conclusion must be his conclusion of the sermon "Óscar Romero: Beatitude Made Flesh":

... death could not hold him. He is not remembered by sorrowful refrains, but by that cheerful one we hear in barrios and churches throughout the Americas: "Óscar Romero, *¡presente!*" "Óscar Romero, *¡presente!*" as the many join him in the good adventure by defending the poor, comforting the mourning, walking with the meek, and securing justice for those to whom it is denied. God knows, it is still a risk to be merciful, to keep one's heart pure, and to make peace with one's enemies. But the much greater risk is to confuse privilege, acclaim, and self-protection with the good life.[4]

After reading this book, I pray that you can affirm, with so many others, "Jorge Lara-Braud, good adventure to you!"

—John Fife

Preface

This book is a personal account of Jorge Lara-Braud's life. During our twenty-two years of marriage, I was the conservator of Jorge's letters, interviews, sermons, and speeches. Since his death in 2008, I have endeavored to weave his own words into a tapestry that tells the story of his remarkable life. I approached his story as if he were writing his own memoir in his final years, because I believed this approach would bring him closer to you, the reader. My hope is that this writing brings him vividly to life for you, connecting his heart to yours, and inspiring you to aim as he did for the seemingly impossible.

—Gretchen Lara-Shartle

The Meaning of Las Bienaventuranzas *and* Bienaventuranza
by José Luis Velazco Medina

"Óscar Romero: Beatitude Made Flesh," Jorge's sermon that is reproduced later in this book, contributes to his meaning of *bienaventuranza*. *Bienaventuranza* is the Spanish word for *beatitude*. *Las bienaventuranzas*, "The Beatitudes," comes from Jesus's "Sermon on the Mount" (Matt. 5:3–12). To follow the Beatitudes means to stand up for those who "hunger for justice" and those who "work for peace" against injustice, in spite of persecution and, in many instances, death. Jesus emphasized that God is concerned with people who are suffering, the poor, and, today we might add, the "immigrants"!

Any good adventure sometimes has as its reward a blessed experience; therefore, people who follow Jesus and the Beatitudes are involved in a "blessed adventure," a *buena ventura*. When Jorge sometimes splits the word *bienaventuranza* into two words *bien* and *aventuranza*, "good" and "adventure," he is emphasizing this aspect of adventure. When Christians, or the Church, "venture" or dare to practice the challenges implied in the Beatitudes, we experience not only a true and blessed "adventure," but often a tough and challenging one. Challenging because one has to suffer the consequences of practicing God's will, as clearly stated by Jesus.

An example of someone who followed the Beatitudes to his ultimate peril is Óscar Arnulfo Romero. Countless times, he risked his life when he stood up for the poor, the oppressed, and the persecuted. One final time, he dared to order the soldiers to disobey their military orders saying: "I beg you, I beseech you, I order you in the name of God: Stop the repression!"[5] A few days later, he was shot in the heart at the very moment he was blessing the bread and wine at a funeral service in a small hospital chapel.

When Jorge attended the funeral of Archbishop Romero, he knew it would be dangerous, but he saw it as an opportunity to be with the suffering people of El Salvador. His experience at the funeral service was not only terrifying but also quite an adventure, albeit a tragic one.

In spite of obvious danger, both Archbishop Romero and Jorge dared to take great risks. May their actions inspire us to engage in such challenging adventures even in the shadow of the cross.

CHAPTER ONE

Ugly Duckling

*Blessed are the meek
for they shall...*
—Matthew 5:5 (IB)

Bien aventuranza! How blessed I have been with "good adventures" throughout my life.

I have often wondered where my adventurous spirit sprang from. Perhaps it was in my blood. Adolfo Braud, my mother's grandfather, was a Frenchman and the captain of a merchant marine ship that sailed from Bordeaux, France, to Baja California in 1875. It took him almost a year to make the journey of 12,500 miles across the Atlantic, around South America via the treacherous Cape Horn, and up the western coast of Mexico to reach Mazatlán, Sinaloa.

Adolfo Braud settled and married in Mazatlán, and in 1878 my mother's father, Adolfo Braud Gameros, was born. Family legend has it that in 1892, when young Adolfo Gameros was fourteen years old, he stowed away on his father's ship, the *Corrington*. His father, the captain, discovered him and, furious at his impudence, threw young Adolfo Gameros into the sea and stalked away to his cabin in a rage. The crew of the ship took pity on the boy, fished him out of the water, and hid him until they made landfall. How could a fourteen-year-old boy have survived such an experience?

But survive he did, for in 1898 at age twenty Adolfo Braud Gameros married my grandmother, Concepcion Wilson, the daughter of a Mexican mother and British immigrant father. Conchita, as my maternal grandmother was known, was only fifteen when she married my grandfather in Mazatlán. Soon they moved to El Dorado, Sinaloa, where my grandfather was employed by the Joaquin Sugar Refinery. He ultimately became the chief of maintenance there.

Adolfo and Conchita lived in a beautiful home on the Calle de Bamboo, and it was here in 1908 that my *mamá*, María Artemisa Lara de Braud, was born. Their house had large arches, or *portales*, and an orchard so big that when the circus came to town they kept their elephants, horses, and other animals in the back yard. There was a patio in the center, where Conchita kept her cow. She and her children would all milk the cow, then drink the warm milk.[1]

Jorge's mother and her sisters with a visiting elephant from the circus in El Dorado.
"Mamá" is the one with short hair in the white dress in front of the elephant.

My *papá*, Luis Lara Castro, was also born in 1908, to Doña Jesusita and Margarito Lara Castro, who were both originally from Mocorito, Sinaloa. As a child, I did not spend as much time with Papá's family, so I know very little about their history. I remember, however, that my grandmother, Doña Jesusita, exemplified her name, and was so full of lovingkindness we thought she was a saint. I hoped to be like her, but always fell short.

Papá studied for four years in a seminary in Culiacán, Sinaloa. There he lived with his godfather, Plateon Sanchez Aldama, and trained as an accountant. He probably chose to study in a seminary to get a good education, not because he intended to become a priest. He then took a job as an accountant with the Joaquin Sugar Refinery in El Dorado, where Mamá's father worked.

Mamá and Papá married in the orchard of Mamá's family home on Calle de Bamboo on February 2, 1929. Papá told me he had to persuade one of the priests from his seminary to come to the family home in Sinaloa in the middle of the night to marry them. Mamá dressed in ordinary clothes, so no one would suspect she was getting married. This was a dangerous time in Mexico, especially for priests.[2]

When I later studied Mexican history, I understood more clearly the reasons for this midnight ceremony. During the Mexican Revolution from 1910 to 1920, more than 90 percent of the priests and bishops in Mexico were murdered, expelled, or left the country voluntarily.[3] By 1933, four years after my parents were married, there were only 197 authorized priests in all of Mexico,[4] compared to 5,000–6,000 priests in the eighteenth century.[5] It is amazing they could find a priest anywhere, and especially one who would marry them when the conflict between the Catholic Church and the government was still so volatile.

My brother, Luis, was born in 1930, a year after my parents married. Soon after his birth, my parents, grandparents, and Mamá's seven younger sisters all moved to Mexicali, the capital of Baja California, and only six blocks south of the California–Mexico border. The area around Mexicali had originally been settled by Spanish Jesuits. The land was harsh and isolated. With a dry, desertlike climate, the area was known for its triple-digit summer temperatures and extremely cold winters. Even the Jesuits gave up and left in the 1780s.

Lara-Braud family
Top left to right: Consuelo, María Magdalena ("Nena"), Delia, Concepción ("Concha"), Enriqueta ("Queta"), Artemisa ("Micha," Jorge's mother). Bottom left to right: Raúl, Concepción ("Conchita," Jorge's grandmother), Ramón.

Despite these drawbacks, people realized the area could be farmed if only an irrigation system could be implemented. The Mexican government was building schools and roads, but its strongest commitment was to the irrigation program, because without water, life was not possible. As evidence of this commitment, the National Commission of Irrigation was established. The commission created an intricate system of dams and continually turned fallow deserts into green gardens. Papá's job as an accountant for the national commission brought our family to Mexicali.

The family celebrated Luis's first birthday, and shortly after, I was born on April 2, 1931, and christened Jorge Lara-Braud. It must have been very trying for Mamá to marry, move from her idyllic childhood home, and have two children in quick succession. No doubt she was overwhelmed, and she simply had little energy left to care for me. I was confused and hurt by her indifference. As I grew older, I became aware I did not look like Mamá and Luis, who both had beautiful porcelain skin, but I more closely resembled Papá with his *café*-toned skin. My skin was the color of maple syrup; my hair was curly and unruly. These things would shape my idea of myself as an "ugly duckling." When Mamá called me her "*prietito*," her (little brown one), she no doubt meant it as an endearment, but it stung me.

Mamá, Jorge (left), and Luis (right)

Feelings of insecurity were exacerbated when my sister, "Cachuy," Maria de Jesus Lara-Braud, was born in 1935. I was in the middle between my handsome, confident older brother, Luis, and my adorable little sister. I was a frightened child, overlooked by people around me as if I were invisible. I cowered behind doors and chairs, with no confidence in my appearance or my abilities.[6]

However, I would soon call upon my courage and speak out in front of my whole school. Having a teacher who believed in me would encourage me to become more self-confident.

CHAPTER TWO

A Season of Discovery

*I had an experience that went
deeply to the root of my identity.*

—Jorge Lara-Braud, "Mi Jornada"

In 1935, when Cachuy was forty days old, I was four, and Luis five, we moved from Mexicali to the state of Chihuahua, where my father worked at a dam called Las Virgenes. The name of the town was Delicias, meaning "delights." It was located on the rail line in the rich Conchos River valley, fifty-two miles from Chihuahua, the state capital. Because area farmers needed rail transport to take their produce from farm to market, Delicias was strategically built close to a major railroad line.

As one of the five original families who had come to Delicias to work for the National Commission of Irrigation, we were allotted a beautiful American-style house. It had a porch at the entrance, a living room, a dining room, a kitchen in the back, and three bedrooms.[7] Even though we were by no means well-off, we lived comfortably.

Through his work for the commission, Papá was loaned a truck to transport cement. When we heard the train horn sounding a special signal, we knew that cement had arrived and had to be quickly unloaded.[8] My father became friends with train workers when he went to pick up the cement. From them he learned they were still haunted by an event that had occurred back in 1927. When the Cristeros, who represented the Catholic Church in its conflict with the government during the Mexican Revolution, dynamited the Mexico City–Guadalajara train, a hundred passengers were killed.[9] Eight years later, Chihuahuans still feared more violence might break out. Though the revolution had ended in 1920, peace was not restored to Chihuahua, and most other parts of Mexico, until the 1930s. Fear of violence prevented many people from moving into unsettled areas like Delicias, which did not officially become a town until January 7, 1935, the year we arrived. Consequently, Delicias was one of Mexico's youngest cities.

Many blamed the unsettled situation in Chihuahua on General Pancho Villa and his followers. Villa was a famed Mexican revolutionary and guerrilla leader who after 1914 engaged in banditry and helped foment civil war. Although he was assassinated in 1923, stories about him and the chieftains who followed him still abounded. The very thought of him terrified some adults. We kids, however, were awed by his image. We felt Chihuahua had been made safer by Villa. As enemies of the Cristeros, Villa and his chieftains had made it practically impossible for the Cristeros to burn schools and harass people in Chihuahua as they had done in other parts of Mexico.

Luis and I idolized him and used to play Pancho Villa games when we went down to the river. At times, others would join us. Luis was always Pancho. The rest of us took orders from him as we pretended to ride our horses across the desert. Then, at the end of our play, Luis, as Pancho, would fall into the water after being shot by one of us. Often, Mamá and Cachuy would come down to join us with a picnic lunch. Those times were magical.

For many years, there had been no school for fifty or sixty miles around Delicias. Because of the considerable amount of violence in the past, many parents were so afraid for their children's safety they chose not to send them to school. After 1931, as peace was reestablished, a semblance of normalcy returned to this part of the country. Fortunately for us, the founders of Delicias were an enlightened group. Like my parents, they believed that having a good school in the town was necessary for our families. They hoped that as the town grew, there would be qualified teachers, workers, and technicians to help it prosper.

Because there had never been a school before, almost everyone was in the first grade, even though our ages ranged from four to sixteen. It was not unusual for me, the youngest, to help a sixteen-year-old girl while sitting in her lap.[10]

At the Delicias school, I had some of the best teachers I ever had in my life, including my graduate years at Princeton. I heard Papá say several times that he would not have agreed to come to Delicias, even for his job, if there had not been a school for the three of us. One could never have guessed this from the reading material available in our home. We owned only one book, and it belonged to me. It was titled *De Los Apininos a Los Andes*, written by an Italian.[11] Even back then, I dreamt of the time when I might have my own special library and be surrounded by books.

In Delicias, we were surrounded with possibilities for learning about the world. Back then, Mexico had neither the necessary technicians nor the technical equipment to match its ambitious plans. Consequently, talent and equipment were imported from other countries; hence, Delicias became a community of at least fourteen nationalities. There were families from the Soviet Union, Poland, Italy, Spain, United Kingdom, and France, even China. Having always been filled with curiosity about the world, I was delighted by the town's cosmopolitan nature.

As long as I can remember, I have loved to learn. Our school was a government-run school with at least one teacher per grade. My teacher, Mrs. Casades, was the first person in my life who believed in me and helped me believe in myself. She was an inspiring teacher and a devoted nationalist, who loved her country, not just in words but in deeds. For example, we painted the classroom with

Aztec symbols so that when you entered the classroom, not only were you met by a flash of light, cultural self-awareness, and pride, but you were also met with something that went deeply to the root of your identity.[12]

Mrs. Casades taught us not to be ashamed of manual work, and to realize we were part of a new generation of Mexican intellectuals. She made this clear. "Your mind is the most valuable gift that you have been given, but you have also been given a pair of hands in order that you might dignify the land, and in so doing, dignify yourselves."[13] And so she taught us to be carpenters, farmers, and pharmacists. She taught us to do many practical things.[14]

She secured from the school a plot of two or three acres. Each of us was given a certain amount of land, and it was up to us to decide what to grow. We had to read books on agriculture. I planted my little plot with beans, and my plants grew luxuriously, with only one problem—there were no beans. Mrs. Casades suggested that I do a little more reading and find out how something could be so impressive, but also impressively barren. The next time around, I grew an equally magnificent crop, but this time it had beans.[15] After that, Mrs. Casades suggested to me that just as I had made these beans grow, I too could grow, begin to speak out, and do special things with my life.

My chance came soon after. In 1941, the U.S. territory of Hawaii had been attacked by the Japanese, and the United States declared war against the Axis powers. I learned that two Mexican oil tankers had been torpedoed and sunk in the Gulf of Mexico. During this time, the United States had been pushing Mexico to become an ally. Although it was later confirmed that German U-boats did in fact sink the Mexican tankers, at the time there were people who swore they had seen the insignia of the U.S. Navy on the submarines. Understandably, this belief led to public outrage. I went to Mrs. Casades and said, "Will you march with me and organize an anti-American protest? We have no business joining the United States, our arch-enemy." Mrs. Casades was absolutely delighted. Although I was very shy, I gave a speech. The speech was miserable, but not the idea of it. Of that, I could be proud.[16]

I was also proud of my leadership role in the demonstration. Looking back at the timid ten-year-old boy that I was, it was daring for me to organize a protest. My willingness to speak out courageously foreshadowed the person I would become.

CHAPTER THREE

From Paradise to the Barrio

*Like any genuine adventure,
it is the confident taking of risk,
the courage to defy the odds,
the refusal to play it safe.*

—Jorge Lara-Braud, "Óscar Romero: Beatitude Made Flesh"

The same year I gave my speech, Mamá, Luis, Cachuy, and I were forced to leave Delicias. My parents had separated because my father had left Mamá for another woman. We traded our idyllic life in Delicias for life on the third floor of a tenement building in Mexico City located on a street named Serapio Rendón where drug use and prostitution were common. The apartment was grim. Luis and I slept in the kitchen and dining area, while Cachuy and Mamá shared a little room adjacent to ours. Outside, there was no place to play. There were parks, but they were littered with refuse.

Jorge on Serapio Rendón Street where he grew up

Despite our bleak living arrangements, Mamá encouraged us to never give up. She kept reminding us that our life on Serapio Rendón was temporary. At the time, I wondered why my mother's family did so little to help us. Now I understand they too were struggling. I also wondered why my father had not helped us. Later I learned he tried to send money, but unfortunately, Mamá was too proud to accept his offers.

The apartment building where Jorge and his family lived in Mexico City

Many of the other mothers turned to prostitution to support their families. Instead, Mamá got a job as a "secretary," a euphemism, for the most part, since her job was to clean offices. She did do some typing, and I taught her spelling. She was forever helping us find ways to rise above these miserable conditions. Although Luis and I only had one coat each, Mamá told us to wear it for school or church every day. She felt that if we were well turned out, people might treat us better. And they did.

18 DARE TO ADVENTURE

We made the best of this situation by becoming connected with people in our building who shared our interests. There were marvelous social events where the neighbors invited each other for food and drink. At these parties, friends and neighbors gathered to sing, to dance, to do whatever they did best. This is how I discovered that I had a beautiful singing voice. In fact, I began to participate in school and neighborhood contests.[17] It was fun to compete—surprisingly, I sometimes won. While winning now seems like a small thing, being recognized, even momentarily, boosted my spirit.

Jorge (12), Mamá, Cachuy (8), and Luis (13) while living in Mexico City

I always felt our situation was precarious. But we began to discover that some of us had personal resources that together could help us to survive. My brother and I sold classified ads to earn money. I remember the first time we did this: Luis with his characteristic decisiveness said, "You take this side of the street and

I'll take that side. Five blocks from here we will meet and find out how we are doing." When we got to the fifth block, I had nothing and he had twenty-five applications for ads. While I rejoiced in my brother's ability to help Mamá, the more he succeeded, the more inadequate I felt.[18]

My school and my church were central to my life in Mexico City. My attraction to Our Lady of Guadalupe and my desire to learn more about God and Jesus drew me to the church. Our Lady of Guadalupe had been a Mexican Indian and is called the "mother of the abandoned ones." There is a famous passage in the Gospel of Luke, the Magnificat, in which the mother of Jesus sings of God coming to pull the mighty down from their thrones and uplift those of low degree. For me, this epitomized the teaching of the Virgin of Guadalupe, that God will help the poor and send the rich away with nothing. The experience of having been abandoned by my own father and left to live in that tenement brought me closer to Our Lady of Guadalupe.

Our family had a saying: "Religion is for women and children." If you were a dedicated Catholic as a boy, you were teased as a sissy. Therefore, if you were religious, you had to hide it. Religion simply would not have won a popularity contest, but at the same time, we would defend with our lives the honor of the Lady of Guadalupe.[19]

At times when I felt lost, I would go to San Cosme Church just around the corner to pray for all of us and find some peace. I loved to kneel before a little statue of Jesus and touch his face, as if he might come alive. I prayed that Mamá could endure this awful humiliation of living in poverty and for Cachuy, Luis, and myself. I spent more time in the church than my brother or any of our friends did. My cousin Memo teased me about being a "prayer boy."[20]

Mamá sent all of us to catechism classes. We liked our Saturday teacher the best. She helped me expand my mind even when I disagreed with what she was teaching. She taught us that God's only begotten son had to die so we could be forgiven for our sins. We were told to believe this and everything we were taught or we might go to hell. This made no sense. How could they teach us that God was both loving and forgiving, yet that same God would still send us to hell? I did not know what hell was, or really if there was a hell. We were not allowed to ask these kinds of questions—or for, that matter, any questions.

After catechism class we proceeded to confess our sins to the priest. Once I learned that Father Manuel and Father José were the most lenient when it came to penances, I looked forward to confession. They were both understanding, so I found it helpful to talk about what I had done wrong and then be forgiven.

Certain things frustrated me, such as being threatened with hell, and being told that singing was reserved for those who spoke Latin. I also found it incomprehensible that we were not allowed to read the Bible on our own. We were told that it was forbidden to laity, because we could not possibly comprehend it. Our teachers said only the priests could understand and explain Scripture. However, I never spoke to the priests about these concerns. Since the situation had been much worse in Mamá's day, she did not share my frustrations with the church.

I began to wonder what had moved church leaders to act this way. I began to understand why in high school, when I learned more about the conflict between the Mexican government and the Catholic Church. In 1917, the government passed laws that allowed the expropriation of church properties and that prohibited priests and Protestant ministers from voting on public policy. Soon after his election in 1924, President Plutarco Elías Calles required state licensing of priests, which meant the state could limit the number of priests by not licensing them. Priests who continued to serve without licenses were forced underground. Consequently, many parts of Mexico, like Sinaloa, where my parents married, were left with no priests at all. Since their landholdings, their wealth, and even the number of priests had been severely diminished, church leaders may have felt one of the few things left to them was their secret access to God. Whatever the reasons may have been, I felt frustrated with my own church.

However, I tried to make the best of a difficult situation. Though I continued to be quietly critical of my catechism classes, I knew this was the only place for me to learn about God and Scripture. The fact that we were not allowed to read the Bible made me wish I could delve into it on my own. While other friends in my catechism class did not seem to care about these restrictions, to me they were upsetting. Regardless, these glimpses of biblical knowledge enticed me to learn more—much more.

Because we were in public school, an additional benefit to catechism classes was meeting other students my age from Catholic schools. One of those friends told me that when the minister of education came to his school, he and the other students were made to hide their books related to church doctrine. Then, when he left, students would take them out and return to their regular religious studies. After talking to my friend, I felt relieved we did not have to play that kind of cat-and-mouse game in my school.

The public school Jorge attended in Mexico City

Another thing the clergy taught us was that Communists were enemies of Christianity. Of course, I could never be persuaded that Mrs. Casades was a bad person because she was a Communist. Although our country was going through an exciting period of nationalistic enthusiasm, any significant insurgency was condemned by the church.

One of the things I liked the most about my public school was that it prepared me to be an internationalist. The experience of living in Delicias gave me my first taste of being a world citizen. In Mexico City, there was also an international dimension to our education. Every Monday morning, before going into our classrooms, we would line up according to our grade level and sing "The Internationale," the anthem of the world communist movement, then the "Mexican National Anthem." Finally, we would sing the "Marseillaise." Singing the "Marseillaise" reminded me I was part French.

I especially remember my sixth-grade teacher. He appreciated the fact that I did well in his class and that he could entrust his students to me when he would take frequent breaks. He was a spiffy, sartorial man who I'm sure would have loved to have been respectable, but alcohol consumed his life. Every few hours, he needed to take leave to take a drink, and then return. That was his life. I became his substitute for these absences of fifteen, twenty, or even thirty minutes. I did so well as a substitute teacher that my class did not object. They often said they preferred my teaching.

My brother, Luis, was so eager to get out of school that he decided not to take his senior-year exams. Since our last names were the same and our classes were large, no one noticed when I took his exams and passed everything, though I had not prepared. This enabled him to receive his high school diploma. While I was happy to help Luis in this way, I felt bad to have been duplicitous. Although I succeeded academically, an area where Luis did not, my family seldom celebrated my successes.

Even though my life in Mexico City was often discouraging, I felt proud of myself for my academic achievements. I was at the top of my class and had even been admitted to the University of Mexico at age fifteen. Also, in a strange way, my experience with the Catholic Church had touched my soul. While I was critical of the church, there were some positive aspects, such as learning about the power of forgiveness through confession. For as long as I can remember, I have been drawn to God; but not until those years in Mexico City did I realize this was an essential part of my being.

However, I felt frustrated and lost. I had no real purpose. Tenement life horrified me, especially our dreadful apartment and having to share the tiny kitchen space for sleeping with Luis, who dominated the space. His personality was so strong that it left little room for me. At the same time, my sister was growing up to be a beautiful girl, astonishingly beautiful. Compared to my sister, I was still an ugly duckling. Caught between the beautiful and the strong, I felt like a socially inadequate nincompoop.[21]

I had no one to turn to. I tried praying but it did not seem to help. One night, I had a wild idea: I could run away. At first, it seemed preposterous. Just a few years before, I was that timid boy hiding behind chairs and doors. Even thinking of such a move would have put me into a panic. Now I was considering leaving the only security I knew—my family. I was petrified but determined not to be governed by my fears.

Jorge shortly before he ran away

I had caught a glimpse of my inner strength when I gave that speech together with Mrs. Casades in Delicias. The international dimension of my own heritage, our lives in Delicias, and our schooling in Mexico City all gave me a taste of the wider world, and I wanted to experience it. More than anything, I was determined to find a purpose for my life.

I kept going back and forth pondering whether I should leave. I hated to hurt Mamá, who was laboring so hard to keep our family together. Each time I thought of leaving her, I felt guilty. But I knew I could not stay. I was desperate. I could not imagine remaining where I was, feeling purposeless, diminished by my brother's extroverted charisma and ashamed of the circumstances that condemned us to poverty.

Lying in bed one night, I finally made my decision. Before dawn on a cold November night in 1946, I ran away from the horrors of our tenement on Serapio Rendón Street and into the unknown.

CHAPTER FOUR

I Stand My Ground

*I came to the conclusion that there is
an existential moment in your life
when you must decide to speak for yourself;
nobody else can speak for you.*

—Martin Luther King Jr.

In order to leave, I needed money. In desperation, I stole from the savings my mother kept in the kitchen. This went against everything inside of me, but I knew of no other way. I went to the railroad station, although I was not sure where to go. After a while, I decided on Delicias. From the train, I sent a wire to my father, whom I had hardly seen since the marriage breakup five years earlier, and asked him to meet me at the railroad station.

I would miss Mamá, knowing she would be the most upset. I would even miss the priests who had listened to our confessions week after week. Already, I wanted to confess and be forgiven not only for stealing money to buy my train ticket, but for leaving so abruptly without telling my family how much I loved them. I yearned to talk with them before leaving; however, if I had, they would not have let me go. I wanted to find my way and knew that meant taking risks. On that train ride it became clear that I had to make something of myself. No one else could do that for me.

I sat on the train for sixteen hours and traveled over seven hundred miles. As we drew closer to Delicias, around 4:30 in the morning, I grew increasingly nervous about seeing Papá. While I did not expect him to welcome me, I hoped he would. Yet, how? Might he be fearful that I was coming to reprimand him for leaving all of us in such dreadful circumstances in Mexico City? He and Marina, his new partner, were probably enduring criticism from our friends in Delicias. No doubt, most of our neighbors would have remained loyal to Mamá since she was the offended one. In Mexican society, the offending party loses most rights to any continuing relationship with his or her children. And since he had begun to see Marina while still married to Mamá, he was definitely seen as the offender.

Here I was, alone at age fifteen. It was very early in the morning and quite chilly. When the train arrived, Papá was on the platform. Instead of welcoming me, he said, "I am taking you to a hotel so that you can sleep, but you are going to be on the train back to Mexico City either tomorrow or the day after. And that is it." He did not even ask me, "Do you want to stay?" I wish he would have. Instead he said, "I am afraid that you will say that you want to stay and it will be very hard on you and very hard on me."[22]

I said, "Why don't we try it? You are not taking me to a hotel. You are taking me to your home."[23]

For the first time in my life, I took a strong stand. Until the moment I ran away, I had obeyed my mother and taken orders from Luis. While I hoped not to alienate Papá, returning to Mexico City would have meant admitting total failure. Even though my surprise arrival troubled him, he finally agreed to take me to his home. He did not want to encourage this break between my mother and me; nor did he want to be seen in a more negative light. Others might think he was taking advantage of me, because I would somehow "legitimize" his infidelity by coming to live with him.

When we arrived at the house, Marina was sitting in the living room holding her sleeping baby, my half-sister, Magaly. My father introduced me, saying that I would be staying in the house for only a few days. I was back in what had been my beloved Delicias, but now it was completely different from the paradise of my childhood. It felt like I was a stranger in what had been my home.

Within a few days after arriving, I began to ask myself, what is the next step from here? I was not going back to Mexico City.[24] I even tried to talk with family friends hoping they would help me find my way. However, they were loyal to Mamá; with one voice, they pressured me to return to Mexico City. After hesitating a few days, I phoned Mamá to tell her where I was. She then started constantly phoning, imploring me to come home. Despite the pleas from Mamá and her friends, I refused to give up and go back to Mexico City.

At first, Marina and I were cool toward each other. I worried about betraying Mamá, and Marina probably felt duty-bound to support Papá. As the days turned into weeks, and Christmas came and went, I was happily surprised to notice my heart was warming to both Marina and Magaly. Later, I dared believe they were also warming to me.

Maybe Marina saw me as another struggler like herself, because we were both lonely. I often felt like an orphan, with my mother far away and my father hesitant to take me in. Because my parents had been among the first settlers in Delicias, long-term residents loyal to Mamá thought of Marina as the *"concubina"* (a term used by both my parents), who had seduced Papá and destroyed our family.[25] At times, I was tempted to whisper to Mamá's friends that they were not helping anyone in our family by treating Marina this way, that years had passed and to please forgive her. But I knew they would not take me seriously. In their eyes, I was only a kid. Strangely, the fact that we both felt excluded made us closer. I had returned as a "runaway," and she was morally blemished in the eyes of people in Delicias.

One cold day in February, I decided to give Marina a boost by offering to prepare lunch. Marina happily accepted my offer, so I cooked lunch while she nursed Magaly. I was a bit nervous but hoped I could remember exactly how to make the refried beans and rice Mamá had taught me to make when we all lived in Delicias. Once I started cooking, I remembered exactly, and they were delicious. My father actually was surprised and even seemed impressed, which delighted me.

Eventually, Marina trusted me to stay with Magaly when she went out to do errands. Usually, Magaly was asleep when she left, but several times she woke up. I learned to change her diaper and began to play with her. Then I started teaching her to walk, coaxing her as she tumbled awkwardly across the room. I came to love my little half-sister. We all celebrated her first birthday together that March. When she blew out her candle, I silently wished for clues to find a clear direction for myself. But I continued to feel lost. There seemed to be no future for me in Delicias.

That July, something wonderful happened. A friend of Papá's had a son who was attending a school in Kingsville, Texas, the Texas Mexican Industrial Institute—Tex-Mex. This young man was spending his summer vacation in Delicias. He gave me literature to read. It was glossy and attractive and included information about religious education. Tex-Mex was a vocational school for people to learn a trade and learn to speak English. This would then open doors far and wide for these students. The school sounded very attractive. Most attractive of all was that I could work my way through school, and only have to pay one hundred dollars in tuition and fees. I could not believe my good fortune.[26]

The brochure explained that the institute had been founded in 1911, thanks to a donation of seven hundred acres by Henrietta King, of the King Ranch family. A Presbyterian minister, James Skinner, had undertaken the building of a school to educate both Mexican and Mexican American boys. While the literature mentioned the Presbyterian Church, I did not know what the word "Presbyterian" meant.

Right away, I realized this was the school for me. I loved the idea of life in a new country. I took the literature to my father and said, "Please, I need funds sufficient to make this happen. I am going to Tex-Mex." I think it is poetic justice that most of the money that it took to go to Tex-Mex came, not from Papá, but from Marina's savings.[27]

Late that summer, when I said goodbye to Magaly and Marina, I told Marina how grateful I was for her help. It was tough to leave them. When Papá took me to the train station, saying goodbye to him was just as hard. We had both grown closer during my stay in Delicias, and I wondered if this might be the last time I would see him, or any of them.

At sixteen, I embarked on a twenty-hour trip to a new country. Although the anticipation of going was exciting, it was daunting. I could barely speak English and did not know anyone in Texas.

During that train ride, I began to reflect on my ten months' stay in Delicias. While difficult at first, it had ended on a positive note. I had felt socially isolated in a place where a few years before I was completely accepted. However, my feelings of isolation may have been good, for they helped to open my heart to Papá and Marina. Now I understood their struggle, because I had lived it.

It helped me to remember I was going toward what I hoped would become my new life. While uncertain, I trusted in God that I was on a good path.

CHAPTER FIVE

The Wellspring

*God knows, it is still a risk
to be merciful, to keep one's
heart pure, and to make peace with
one's enemies.*

—Jorge Lara-Braud, "Óscar Romero: Beatitude Made Flesh"

On a Thursday afternoon in mid-September 1947, I was on a train en route to a strange country. I was about to arrive in Kingsville, Texas. Papá had sent a telegram to the school with the time my train would arrive, but what if no one came? The closer the train got to Kingsville, the more fearful I became. I had only ten dollars, and I had no idea where the school was. I prayed someone would meet me. Thank goodness! There was a woman with her arms outstretched saying to me as I got off the train, "You must be Jorge Lara-Braud. I am Mrs. Cobbs." I was so grateful, but still uncertain about what I had gotten myself into. Then, to my mortification, I had to go to the bathroom. Mrs. Cobbs pointed me to a place indicated by a sign that read, "Mexicans only." I was appalled. Could there be such a thing?

Being with Mrs. Cobbs turned out to be a blessing. She was full of cheer and wanted to hear all about my trip, so I told her about it as well as I could in my halting English. The school was only five miles from the Kingsville train station. We arrived quickly, and she took me to my dormitory, a dilapidated building that looked like it was about to collapse. I was assigned my own room on the second floor. The bathroom was downstairs, which proved to be a challenge on cold winter nights.

Soon after arriving, I realized I had set foot in the land of my church's deadly enemies—the Protestants! Though I had read that Tex-Mex was a "Presbyterian" school, I had assumed Presbyterians were a civic group akin to Rotarians or the Lions Club. Not only had fear and loathing of Protestants been instilled in us at church; it penetrated our daily lives. Throughout Mexico, signs at the entrance of many homes read: "*Este es un hogar católico; rechazamos toda propaganda comunista y protestante*" (This is a Catholic home; we reject all Communist and Protestant propaganda).[28]

Mrs. Marjorie Cobbs[29]

I settled in for a long siege. I would have to learn how to take advantage of an American education, while saving my soul from the lures of Protestantism and the pressures of my mentors. With gritted teeth and clenched fists, I began to comply with chapel attendance, daily Bible classes, and the Sunday worship services.[30]

After chapel following my arrival, the school held an orientation session for new students. The meeting was headed by President McLane, and many faculty attended. We students were told about our class and work schedules. That's when I met Mr. Perry Reed, with whom I would be studying English and world history three days a week, and learned that Mrs. Cobbs would be teaching me Bible, something that would have been unheard of in Mexico. Since we were required to do manual work every day and Saturday mornings, I signed up to help in the dining room during the week, then to work with Mrs. Cobbs's husband, who ran the farm on Saturdays. From him, I learned how to repair cars and farm machinery. I liked the mix between manual and academic work.

Main building of the Texas Mexican Industrial Institute when Jorge attended school

Because of my inability to write and speak English, the school placed me in the seventh grade. Since I had already been admitted to the University of Mexico the year before, this was humiliating.

After a few months, I slowly began to relax and even started to glimpse some goodness in my teachers. Mrs. Cobbs was one of my favorites. She was gifted with a buoyancy that was contagious. Beyond that, she also did everything in her power to expose me to good music and good books. She conveyed to me the clear idea that I was going to go places.[31]

Mr. Cobbs

At the time, I had no clear idea where or what those places might be. For a brief period, I had secretly hoped to become a nightclub singer. Even more, I hoped I might use my intelligence to discover a new kind of medicine that would help save lives. Though still uncertain, I began to believe that someday I would likely become engaged in helping impoverished people.

One of the first things that opened my heart was the singing. I quickly learned dozens of Protestant hymns. I felt close to heaven when we sang hymns like "Joyful, Joyful, We Adore Thee" and "*Jesus es mi Rey Soberano.*"[32] I would sing my heart out without regard for Calvinist propriety, sometimes drawing startled looks. I also began to enjoy listening to thought-provoking sermons.

Whether in Spanish or English, I was attracted to beautiful language. This is why I listened carefully to the way my teachers spoke and appreciated signs of eloquence in our chapel sermons. Eventually, I even decided to forgive the Chicano and Gringo preachers who spoke to us in flawed Spanish. I suspected they were invited by the school to improve the chances of our conversion, which was affront enough. But to hear them murder Spanish, my language, the language of God and the angels, was at first more than I could bear.[33]

By my second year at Tex-Mex, I started to feel a sense of belonging. In one year, I moved from seventh grade to eleventh grade. I played first base on the school baseball team and helped form a vocal quartet that went on promotional tours for the school. We sang in churches throughout South Texas, gave individual testimonies, and spoke about our lives at the school. That is when it began to occur to me that someday I might even consider becoming a Presbyterian.

I was attracted to the Presbyterian Church for many reasons, but I was still hesitant to embrace a group I had been taught to reject. As I pondered this decision night after night, Bible stories comforted me. It helped me to realize that Jesus had a big embrace. He did not seek perfection when he chose his followers. He chose ordinary human beings, people who often failed as I had—people not unlike me.

Identifying with people in Scripture was a source of hope in my daily life. What a contrast to my catechism classes in Mexico City, where we had been threatened over and over with hell. However, through reading the Bible at Tex-Mex, I found a sense of acceptance for my true self. As I read the story of Moses leading the Hebrews from oppression to the land of freedom, I became one of those Hebrew boys trudging across the Mexican desert to a new land in America. I loved the story of Jacob and his dream of angels coming to him on a ladder from heaven. I believed this was God's way of forgiving Jacob, who had tricked his brother, Esau. Esau then greeted Jacob and hugged him. I continued to be troubled about having left my mother, brother, and sister in Mexico City so abruptly, and hoped I could be forgiven as Jacob was.

The more I read about Jesus, the more I loved him, and the more I felt loved by God because of him. What enthralled me most was his life and ministry. He lived out the presence of God as a thoroughly compassionate human being, whose predilection was always for the most vulnerable. I learned about God's preferential love for the poor, the orphans, and the widows, and God's determination to establish his gracious rule of love and justice here on earth. Talk about revelation, of course, it was! It was the word of God.[34] This was the word I had been told only priests could read and understand.

In addition to being encouraged to read the Bible, I was impressed by the prominent role played by the laity in Presbyterian church governance. I saw this as an expression of equality and democracy: Christians taking responsibility themselves, rather than entrusting their lives to a hierarchy of priests and bishops. Jesus would have loved watching as laypeople performed works of mercy, led worship, and preached the word of God.

Both in my mind and in my heart, I decided I really wanted to become a Presbyterian, but I didn't know how to work it out. The biggest obstacle was my loyalty to Mamá. When I was lying in bed at night, I sometimes saw her face. I was concerned not only for her but for me. I loved her so very much, I did not want to lose her. I knew it would be devastating for her to know I might be thinking of joining a Protestant church. For her, Protestants were enemies. If she thought that in addition to running away, I had also become a Protestant, it might break her heart. I did not want to hurt her; nor did I want to put more distance between us.

For Mamá's sake and mine, I searched for a solution to this dilemma. I needed to speak about this conflict with someone I trusted. While I tended to be introverted and hesitant to tell others about my inner struggles, I finally decided to open up to Bob Bidwell, my teacher of English literature. I found an ideal time to talk with him when we were driving to Corpus Christi for a concert. The other students who often accompanied us could not come that afternoon. So that was my chance to talk privately with Mr. Bidwell. I told him I was warming up to the Presbyterian Church for many reasons. One of the main things that attracted me was the openness.

The Bible had become my own personal wellspring of belief. He understood that since the Bible had been forbidden to us by the Catholic Church in Mexico, I relished it all the more. I told him how wonderful it was to find at Tex-Mex we were not only allowed but encouraged to read the Bible. That is when a new world opened to me. I used it to find my way by myself, rather than following what others might tell me to believe.

The biggest challenge for me was how to remain loyal to my Catholic upbringing and my family while also becoming a Protestant. Bob Bidwell thought for a few minutes then asked me to consider in my heart of hearts what I would like to do. I told him that I wanted to become a Presbyterian without leaving the Catholic Church. He then asked if I found anything objectionable about the Protestant church. Right away, I answered that I wished it was not so intolerant of Catholicism. Mr. Bidwell understood my desire not to hurt Mamá. He told me to think about it and suggested we could talk again in a few months.

During that period when I was agonizing over the thought of hurting Mamá, I prayed for a solution. After studying Luther and Calvin, I had an epiphany. It seemed they had chosen not to make a total break with the Catholic Church. In a similar way, I began to imagine that becoming a Presbyterian would be like joining a reform movement. That way, I could embrace both churches. This synthesis buoyed me up emotionally and intellectually.

Since Mr. Bidwell was the only person I had spoken with about my dilemma, one evening I went over to his apartment and knocked on his door. Luckily, he was there. I told him that, like Luther and Calvin, I wanted to become a Protestant without making a total break from the Catholic Church. I asked if he thought this was too idealistic. He saw no reason why I should hesitate to go forward with this new approach. More than anyone else, Mr. Bidwell encouraged me to feel at ease about my decision. Finally, after being at Tex-Mex for a year, when I was seventeen years old, I decided to become a Presbyterian.

CHAPTER SIX

Moved to Boldness

*Good adventure to you
whose hearts are genuinely with the poor:
you are under God's protective rule.*

—Jorge Lara-Braud, "Óscar
Romero: Beatitude Made Flesh"

What continued to bring the Bible stories to life were my Sunday night visits to the Kleberg County Jail. From my junior year on, our chaplain and Bible teacher, Mr. Jarvis, invited a group of us to go with him to the jail to read the Bible to the prisoners. One particular Sunday, unable to go himself, Mr. Jarvis asked me to lead the group. That evening the reading featured the story of a spontaneous baptism, as told in the Book of Acts 16:19–34.

Kleberg County Courthouse and Jail[35]

According to the story, while in Philippi, Macedonia, Paul and Silas had been beaten, then thrown into prison. That same night, the prison doors mysteriously opened and the prisoners' chains were unlocked. The jailer, seeing what had happened, feared he would be punished and planned to kill himself.

But Paul shouted in a loud voice, "Do not harm yourself, for we are all here." The jailer called for lights, and rushing in, he fell down trembling before Paul and Silas. Then he brought them outside and said, "Sirs, what must I do to be saved?" They answered, "Believe in the Lord Jesus, and you will be saved, you and your household." They spoke the word of the Lord to him and to all who were in his house. At the same hour of the night, he took them and washed their wounds; then he and his entire family were baptized without delay. He brought them up into the house and set food before them; and he and his entire household rejoiced that he had become a believer in God.[36]

After I read this passage from the Bible, the prisoners were so moved by the reading that they asked me to baptize them. Since I was not ordained, I told them I did not have the right to do this. The prisoners argued that the baptism in the Bible reading featured spontaneous baptisms done outside a church setting, and they wanted to be baptized like the jailer and his family in the Bible story. They were so persuasive that I relented. I got a basin from the jail kitchen, filled it with water, then baptized all twenty-five or so prisoners.

While Paul and Silas were physically freed from prison, my freedom was less visible. Nevertheless, it was just as profound. Through embracing Scripture, I was beginning to understand the power of forgiveness and was becoming free of the guilt for hurting Mamá. By daring to follow my heart and act courageously by baptizing the prisoners, I was also becoming free of the timidity that had held me back. Paul and Silas inspired me to realize I too could take big risks.

I wondered if, like Paul and Silas, I might have the courage to continue risking my own well-being to help others. That Sunday night, my choice had been for the underdogs—the prisoners—most of whom were Mexican immigrants. This was my first experience being the underdog caring for underdogs. I had made a quick decision whether to take a risk and baptize the prisoners or follow set rules established by the church hierarchy. Everyone knew that baptism was a ritual to be performed only by pastors.

Since I was a junior in high school with few resources, if the chaplain had decided to admonish me, that could have nixed my chances for college. Being centered in God empowered me to take a huge risk. That evening, in the Kleberg County Jail, I had chosen to follow my inner spirit and the Bible, and I have tried to do that ever since.

During the spring of my senior year, I had another compelling experience that has stayed with me forever. This occurred when returning from a promotional tour with our vocal quartet. We had stopped in Wharton, Texas, to go to a movie.

Bill Jarvis, 1954[37]

Bill Jarvis, our Bible teacher, stopped the car in front of the theater and said, "Men, I hope you will forgive me. My girlfriend lives here. She is a nurse, and I promised I would spend at least an hour with her, because I knew you were going to be understanding. Am I right or wrong?"

We said, "You are right."

So he said, "You go into the theater and when you come out, if I am not there to pick you up, you can go next door to the café." That's what happened. We came out of the theater. Then we went into the restaurant and had to wait a long time to be acknowledged.

Finally, I stopped the waitress and said, "Would it be possible to serve us? We have been here a long, long time."

She blushed and said, "Sorry, fellas, we don't serve Mexicans here." That was shattering because I had been in this bubble of innocence at Tex-Mex, and even when we left the school compound we were constantly in the company of church people. But here we had no one to protect us.

We were walking up and down the curb when our teacher arrived. He asked us what was wrong. I told him and he was mortified. He said, "No, no, no. This should never happen to anyone, and it should certainly not happen to you. Let's get in the car and leave."

I said, "No! We need to do something about this so it will not happen to anyone else. If I am not mistaken, the son of our school president is the pastor of the First Presbyterian Church here in Wharton. Why don't we go by his home and figure out how to deal with this?"

He said, "No, no, no. We are Christians. We do not create conflict. We heal conflict."

And I said, "How do we heal conflict?"

He said, "We will pray about them and we will pray for them. The important thing is to be ambassadors for peace and ambassadors for Christ."

I was very unhappy with that response, and I was even more upset when one of the four of us, the only Mexican American, broke the silence saying, "I don't know why you guys are taking it so hard. This has happened many times. It is going to happen again, so why be so unhappy about it?"

I grabbed him by the lapel and said, "Don't you ever say that again. We will never change things as long as we have this kind of resignation. I am very unhappy with you." There was silence. So we drove another twenty or twenty-five miles in silence. That was the single most influential experience I had in dealing with prejudice, and it happened under the sponsorship, as it were, of Tex-Mex.[38] Surprisingly, the indignity of this rejection was one of the best things that ever happened to me. It gave me a profound sense of identification with the rejected of this world.

I realize my teacher was seeking the veneer of peace, whereas I was aiming for a deeply rooted peace based on mutual respect. He wanted us to leave quietly and just be nice. I'm not sure I fully realized it then, but that day was a turning point for me. I made a decision to speak out against injustice. I realized things would never change if we are just quiet and nice. That decision changed the course of my life.

During those years at Tex-Mex, I had begun to find my way. While in my family I had sometimes felt almost invisible, at Tex-Mex I had found ways to shine. Mr. and Mrs. Cobbs had given me a sense of family. The Gospels had become an added source of strength for me. My fiery spirit was inspired by Jesus. Like him, it helped me to go off, to be alone and pray, when I was feeling tired and overwhelmed. Learning that I could be on my own, and even cherish it, was a great gift. It is one of the best gifts life can offer us.

When I graduated from Tex-Mex in the spring of 1950, I was sad that Mamá, Luis, and Cachuy were not with me. However, I felt grateful that the Cobbs family were there to cheer me on. Joining the Presbyterian Church and acquiring a new family helped to ease my pain, especially when Marjorie Cobbs's son, Stan, asked if he could become my American brother. I knew I would miss them and the school that had nurtured me for three and a half years. I graduated with top honors and received a full scholarship to Austin College. Finally, I was no longer running away but actively heading toward my future.

CHAPTER SEVEN

My Dream

*... with the eyes of your heart enlightened,
you may know what is the hope ...*
—Ephesians 1:18 (NRSV)

In the fall of 1950, once again I set out alone—this time to Austin College in Sherman, Texas, about sixty miles north of Dallas. Through a special arrangement with Tex-Mex, the college had offered me a full four-year scholarship. While I was thrilled to be attending Austin College, it was my only choice. It would have been difficult for me to get such a scholarship at any other college or university. From the start, I was determined to excel academically, as I had at Tex-Mex, but I soon saw how challenging that would be.

In the beginning, I struggled with a profound sense of loneliness. I missed my family, my friends, and my teachers at Tex-Mex. Practically everyone in my class was from Texas and had a family nearby. While they all went home or invited friends for Thanksgiving and Christmas, I felt lost during vacations. Although I was grateful to have a job driving a school bus, this work was another way I was set apart from others.

Speaking English clearly with friends and addressing the public were a challenge. Hardly anyone at Austin College spoke Spanish. Though I understood almost everything, I felt out of place. From the very beginning of my time in the States, I had been determined to improve my English. However at Tex-Mex, Mexicans were so numerous that we learned to speak English mostly from one another. Not surprisingly, we came out speaking like the "Frito Bandito."[39]

Consequently, I was extremely nervous when I had to give my first sermon during my second year of college. Genie Hopper, an educational volunteer who helped link student pastors to needy churches, asked me to serve as lay pastor for a little Presbyterian church thirty miles over the border in Durant, Oklahoma. The Palm Sunday sermon was on Jesus's triumphant entry into Jerusalem.

I was hoping there would be no distractions because of my accent, so the whole week before the service, I went up and down the sidewalks of the college practicing the sound of the "hard d," a sound that doesn't exist in the Spanish language. It was important to master that sound because of the donkey Jesus rode as he entered Jerusalem. I went about saying, "d-d-d-donkey," and the college people would look at me wondering, "What in the world?" Though I had been practicing saying "donkey" all week, I ended up saying, "Even in this great moment of victory, he remains the picture of humility. Look! Look at Jesus riding on the back of a *monkey*." I thought they were spellbound, but they were aghast because I said "monkey," instead of "donkey."[40]

By my second or third year in college, I decided to use the example of one of my teachers as a vocal role model. The one who spoke most clearly was a Scotsman, who split vowels and crackled consonants. By the time I graduated from the college, I sounded like a Mexican farmworker with a polished Scottish accent.[41]

Improving my English had been an important key to being accepted. By my junior year, I was even elected junior class president. Many, including me, were amazed! Not only was I a bus driver—which was unusual in itself—but also the only Hispanic in our class.

In 1954, I was delighted to graduate with honors in philosophy and religious studies. I left Sherman with a clear sense of my hope for the future—a dream I had begun to form early in my freshman year. I first spoke about this dream while in the college choir.

Austin College A Capella Choir
Ruth—Second row, second person from left
Jorge—Third row, third person from left

I traveled with the choir to sing in churches throughout the state. After performing at the First Presbyterian Church in Harlingen, five hundred miles to the south, we gathered at the pastor's home. There I met his son, Mike Murray, who was a high school freshman. While the rest of the choir members enjoyed themselves inventing and performing on-the-spot operettas and dressing in clothes from the 1920s they found in a closet, Mike and I sat in a corner talking of the future. That's when he asked me what I planned to do when I graduated. Without blinking an eye, I announced that I intended to become dean of the Presbyterian seminary in Mexico City. He looked shocked. I could tell by his face that even he, a freshman in high school, thought my aspirations were beyond my reach.

My intention to become dean had begun quietly while I was at Tex-Mex. It was my devotion to Jesus and Scripture that inspired me to become a theologian. As dean, I would have more influence in the theological community, which might allow me to realize some of my more far-reaching ideals like spreading my love of Scripture to others and building bridges of mutual respect between Protestants and Catholics. Also, I wanted to work and live in Mexico City close to my family. I eventually realized my idea to become dean of the Presbyterian seminary in Mexico City may have been beyond my reach because, after graduating from college, I would need not only a degree from a seminary but a higher degree as well. And that path was a financial impossibility.

I left Austin College not only with my dream but also with a wife, whom I had met at Tex-Mex. Sixty miles away from Tex-Mex, there was a school for girls popularly called "Pres-Mex." Every year at Thanksgiving, the boys went to the girls' school, and once in the spring, the girls came to Tex-Mex. Romances began to bud as a result of these one-day visits. I met Ruth Marroquín during one of these visits. She and I were presidents of our respective student councils. Everyone who knew us was so delighted that we were falling in love. Ruth was the daughter of stern, fourth-generation Mexican Presbyterians. Because my family was Catholic, Ruth's father, who was closed-minded about the Catholic Church, was displeased about Ruth becoming my girlfriend.[42]

After Pres-Mex, Ruth went to Belhaven, a women's college in Jackson, Mississippi. Then, the spring of my junior year, she wrote inviting me to visit. Soon after arriving, she asked me to marry her at the end of our junior year. I was stunned. Because I was yearning for a sense of family and rootedness, I agreed, though with some hesitation. Bob Bidwell, my favorite teacher from Tex-Mex, was marrying Ruth's sister, Noemi, in June. Ruth thought it would be wonderful to have a double wedding. She also suggested she could attend Austin College in Sherman her senior year.

Our wedding would be in Mexico City. I was on edge. Here I was not only embracing the Presbyterian faith but marrying into a deeply traditional Protestant family. I had hardly seen Mamá, Luis, and Cachuy since running away seven years before and wondered if they might still be angry with me. Though in my heart I knew they would always love me, I was nervous.

My concerns disappeared, however, when my whole family joined me and the Marroquíns in attending our double wedding held in Príncipe de Paz Presbyterian Church on June 6, 1953, in Mexico City. After the ceremony, our families all celebrated together. At the end of that summer, Ruth returned with me to Austin College, where we graduated together the following year.

Austin College senior yearbook photo, 1954[43]

After graduating, we were uncertain about our next steps. Although I was hesitant, we decided to go to Mexico to work and live that fall. I got a job teaching English to children of wealthy parents at a bilingual college, El Colegio de México. However, I felt uneasy. This plan was not moving me toward my life's purpose. Teaching English did not interest me. I was paid poorly and wasting time.

I temporarily consoled myself with the happiness that came to both Ruth and me with the birth of our son, Jorge Luis (Jorgito), in June 1955. Celebrations in Ruth's family and mine gave me a glimpse of the rootedness I had so sorely missed. For the time being, those ties anchored us in Mexico, where Ruth wanted to remain. I was twenty-five and anxious. How could I go forward with my dream? What if no seminary accepted me? What if I couldn't get a scholarship?

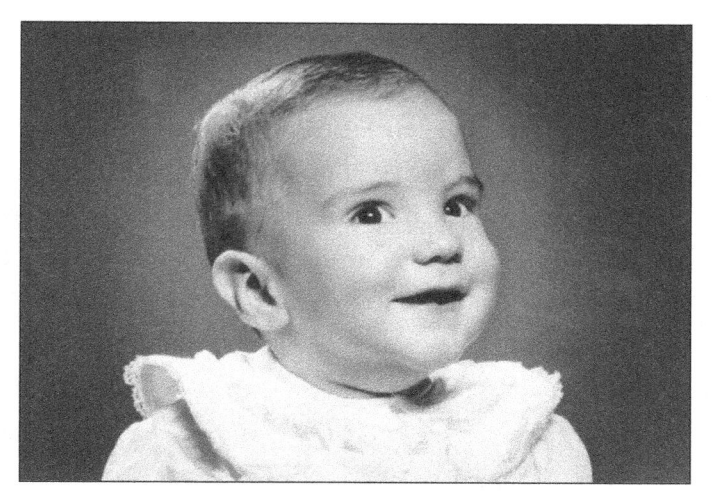

Jorge Luis at one year

Early in 1956, I was inspired by a revolutionary spirit when my church asked me to be a member of a reception committee for Dr. Cecilio Arrastía and Ernesto "Che" Guevara. Dr. Arrastía, a well-known Cuban evangelist, was engaged in planning the overthrow of Fulgencio Batista, the Cuban dictator. Che Guevara was an Argentinian medical doctor who would play a pivotal role in the Cuban Revolution.[44] When our committee met them, none of us realized Dr. Arrastía had ten thousand dollars in cash sewn into the lining of his coat.[45]

That money was two-thirds of what they needed to buy the *Granma*, an old sixty-foot leaky cabin cruiser designed to hold between twelve to twenty-five people at the maximum. On

November 25, 1956, at one in the morning, Che Guevara and Cecilio Arrastía, together with food, weapons, and eighty other revolutionaries, surreptitiously met in Veracruz, Mexico; then they all clandestinely crammed into the *Granma*. That night they set sail and began the 900-mile voyage from Veracruz to Cuba.[46] There they joined other revolutionaries. In this way, I became a witness to the beginning of the Cuban Revolution.[47]

Che Guevara was an inspiration. His dynamic spirit was unlike any I had before experienced. He spoke passionately against Batista's regime. He was horrified by the brutality of the police and Batista's indifference to the needs of the people.[48] He spoke about the plethora of prostitutes and brothels in Cuba and showed compassion for women who supported themselves in that way. After meeting Che, I became even more determined to follow my own dream. To do that, I realized my next step was to attend a top-notch seminary, probably in the United States, despite my lack of monetary support.

In the spring of 1956, I was close to losing hope that I would ever become dean. Then Genie Hopper, who had worked with me in Durant, Oklahoma, arrived in Mexico City with a group on a mission tour from the Austin Presbyterian Theological Seminary.[49] When they came to my church, I was asked to tell them what it meant to be a Protestant in a Roman Catholic country. I told them that while I was a Presbyterian, I also embraced Catholicism. I explained that being at Tex-Mex and having my own Bible had changed my life. As a result, I wanted to delve more deeply into Scripture. They were surprised to hear my dream was to graduate from a seminary and after completing my doctorate to become dean of the Presbyterian seminary in Mexico City.

The seminarians, together with one or two of their teachers, talked to the dean of the seminary when they returned to Austin and suggested they invite me to do a masters of divinity program. Sure enough, within days I got a letter from Dean James McCord saying, "You come and don't worry about money. You will have a full scholarship, and we will find other sources to make sure you are not distracted by the necessity of support for yourself and your family."[50] This felt like a blessing from God. I often wondered why I received these generous gifts. Perhaps it was because churches wanted to assist minorities. It helped that I had performed well academically through the years.

Ruth, Jorge Luis, and I arrived in Austin during the fall of 1956. The seminary asked me—as they asked all of us who were beginning our studies—to decide whether we would eventually want to become ordained ministers of the Presbyterian Church. I explained that because I planned to return to Mexico City to serve the seminary there, I would prefer to remain a theologian. Because I had been imbued with American principles of democracy and encouraged to express my opinions far more freely than in Mexico, my life was dedicated to speaking out. But in Mexico's 1917 Constitution (which was still in effect) it was stated that neither Protestant ministers nor Catholic priests were allowed to vote or speak out about political issues.[51] Consequently, to guard my right to express my views in Mexico, I would need to remain a layperson.

I loved my studies. The seminary was an oasis in the midst of a more conservative Texas. It thrilled me that the professors were so cosmopolitan. Every year the seminary invited outstanding scholars, both American and European, as visiting professors. Now and then, I was asked to teach. I was pleased when, on more than one occasion, Dean McCord would look in on a class of mine and upon hearing what I had to say, would comment, "Not bad; not bad at all." That expression was his highest accolade.

In 1956, Tex-Mex merged with Pres-Mex and the school was renamed the Presbyterian Pan American School. It was during a visit there in the summer of 1957 that I met Dr. John Mackay, the president of Princeton Theological Seminary. I warmed up to him, in part because John, though a Scot, spoke perfect Spanish. Also, it heartened me that he, like me, wanted to further ecumenism—to build a closer understanding between Protestants and Catholics.

Upon graduation from seminary in 1959, I applied to Princeton Theological Seminary and the University of Edinburgh. I was excited when the University of Edinburgh awarded me a full scholarship. There I would be able to complete the classes for my doctorate in one year. However, Ruth was unwilling to move that far from Mexico, so I reluctantly agreed to attend Princeton and was surprised when it too offered to grant me a full scholarship. James McCord, who was in the midst of moving from Austin Presbyterian Theological Seminary to become the dean at Princeton Theological Seminary, may have put in a good word.

The faculty at Princeton was also superb. It attracted European scholars on a temporary basis. For example, I had a professor of Old Testament and Hebrew who was a former Roman Catholic priest of considerable importance in theological circles at the time. I had a British professor of philosophy and a professor of world mission and evangelism from Ceylon (now Sri Lanka).[52]

Most importantly, my first two years there helped me clarify my focus—the relationship between God and the poor as illustrated in the Bible. Whenever I studied the Bible as a source of understanding the Christian faith, I went to the eighth-century B.C.

prophets—Jeremiah, Micah, and Amos—all three of whom spoke movingly about the struggles of the poor. Even in high school, I had memorized parts of these books.

While at Princeton, I worked as a church organizer in Brooklyn. It was there I identified the subject of my doctoral thesis and began work on it during my third year. The title of my thesis was "The Justification for a Protestant Mission to Latin America in the 19th Century."[53] This research, I felt, would give me a deeper understanding of Protestants' involvement in Latin America. Until that point in time, the focus of most scholarly study was on Catholic missionary work. Almost no one had delved into the importance of Protestant missions. This topic would also help me prepare for my work as a Protestant in Mexico.

Jorge Luis, four and a half years old, December 1959, Princeton, N.J.

Jorge Luis, February 1960, Princeton, N.J.

At Princeton, I never forgot my hope to return to Mexico City and serve as dean of the Presbyterian seminary after completing my doctorate. More than once, I had expressed this desire to Ruth's father, Señor Hazael Marroquín, who had close ties to the seminary's administration. He was an important Presbyterian layman and top administrator of the American Bible Society.[54] Largely through his influence, in the spring of 1962, I received a letter from the National Presbyterian Seminary of Mexico offering me the deanship.

The letter jolted me. I say "jolted" because I was not prepared for this opportunity. I needed one more year to complete my doctorate. The offer put me in a bind. While thrilled to have been chosen as dean, when I was only thirty-one and had no experience as a professor, I lamented the fact I had not yet completed my thesis.

I had spent six years leading up to this moment. In one more year, I would have my degree. My choice to be a theologian instead of an ordained minister meant a doctorate would be important for my career as a seminary professor. Dean McCord urged me to stay and graduate. But Ruth was adamant that we should accept the position. Finally, I relented and accepted, but later I came to regret that decision.

CHAPTER EIGHT

My Divided Heart

*Above all, clothe yourselves with love,
which binds everything together in perfect harmony.
And let the peace of Christ rule in your hearts.*
—Colossians 3:14–15 (NRSV)

Full of hope, we arrived in Mexico City in June 1962, for the beginning of my tenure as dean of the National Presbyterian Seminary of Mexico. The academic year ran from early February to late November. The second semester of classes would begin in July.

Once there, our first step was to settle in and spend time with our families. Ruth and I found a lovely two-story house. We rented it together with Ruth's sister, Noemi, and her husband, Bob Bidwell, along with their two children, ages six and two. Our home was located three blocks from the Pan-American Workshop, where Jorge Luis, at age seven, would begin first grade and Ruth would teach fourth grade. The school was near the seminary and both of our families' homes.

In Mexico City
Hector Zavaleta's mother (Hector would marry Genie Hopper), Noemi (Ruth's sister), Bob Bidwell, Hector's Aunt Pearla with her young son, Hector, and Jorge

Early that September my brother-in-law, Jorge Espino, called to tell me that Cachuy had safely given birth to their fifth child, a baby girl named Martha. Cachuy and Jorge Espino's four other children were Lety, Roberto, Carlos, and Jorge Jr. We visited the following Sunday, and I was overjoyed to hold Martha and see my son playing outside with his cousins. My life had come full circle, and I was once again part of my family. Later, when Cachuy called and asked me to be Martha's godfather, I was gratified.

The baptism was held the morning of December 8 in my sister's family church, Santa Maria de la Anunciación. During the service, Jorge Luis stayed close and paid careful attention. He was then a tall, good-looking seven-year-old; he watched with wide brown eyes as the priest lovingly cradled tiny baby Martha. When the priest held her over the baptismal font in the house chapel, then poured water from the font onto her tiny head, my mind wandered. I thought of Jesus's baptism and imagined an inaudible voice: "You are my Son, the Beloved; with you I am well pleased."[55] Yes, Martha was the light of the world, smiling and blessing those around her. Then I gazed at my son and felt proud of him.

During this same period, I was designing a curriculum for my classes at the seminary that I hoped would be approved in October by the church's General Assembly. I was teaching two courses to six graduating seniors, one on Calvin's *Institutes of the Christian Religion*, offered for the first time in the history of the seminary, and another on New Testament theology. What a joy it was to see my students' faces light up in class as we discussed and deliberated theology.[56]

I was so engaged in teaching and spending time with family that at first I did not foresee how challenging it would be for me to fit into the narrower theological world of the Presbyterian Church in Mexico. My seminary studies in Austin and Princeton had included writings by Jewish, Protestant, and Catholic theologians. I never deemed one group superior or inferior to the other. However, early on I noticed a fearful atmosphere at the seminary that was at odds with a positive learning environment—even contrary to the peace of Christ. For example, my students had never been permitted to see secular plays. By condemning theater so totally, I felt the church was unreasonably limiting seminarians and laypeople. I felt it was wrong for church leaders to be so authoritarian, as though only they knew "true morality." Future church leaders needed to understand actual human dilemmas, as portrayed in plays like *A Man for All Seasons*, which tells the story of Sir Thomas More, the highly respected (sixteenth-century) English statesman. When More stood by his religious principles and refused to pressure the pope into annulling the first marriage of King Henry VIII, he was beheaded. Expanding our students' horizons was essential.

In early September, I received a special hand-delivered invitation from Bishop Sergio Méndez Arceo of Cuernavaca, who was the most progressive Catholic bishop of the time. He invited me and four other Protestants to meet with him at his cathedral. He asked that, instead of bringing our books, we bring our experience teaching the Bible in local congregations.[57]

Toward the end of our meeting, the other Protestant representatives told the bishop it was too dangerous for them to meet with him again. They feared being censured by leaders in the church or members of their own congregations. This was my first intimation of just how risky it was for me, as dean of the Protestant seminary, to meet with a Catholic bishop. However, my ideals were stronger than my apprehension; so I decided to follow my heart and chose what I thought was right, rather than be held back by fear.

Soon after our meeting, as part of my new job, I was asked to serve as the liaison between my seminary and three other seminaries in the city: Baptist, Lutheran, and Union Theological. The latter included Methodists, Congregationalists, and Disciples of Christ. In February 1963, I joined leaders from those seminaries, as well as Episcopalians, to discuss our common problems and various ways seminary faculty members might become more effective professors and leaders. We decided to form a regional association of theological institutions and to plan for the creation of a local theological community. In this future ecumenical community, each seminary would preserve its own autonomy while sharing common buildings, such as classrooms, auditoriums, libraries, and chapels. The group asked me to serve as chair of the newly created Association of Theological Seminaries and Bible Schools in Latin America.[58]

Building Christian unity by bringing different denominations together was close to my heart. I asked my church's General Assembly if I could appeal to the Presbyterian Church in the United States to raise the funds we needed for the ecumenical community. Unfortunately, while most other denominations were supported by their U.S. counterparts, in October 1963 my church, the National Presbyterian Church of Mexico, rejected my appeal to ask for funding. I continued to serve as chairman for this group until 1964.

That fall, I saw Bishop Méndez Arceo again when he preached in Mexico City. After the Mass, he invited me to speak in early April at their first annual "Sunday of the Bible" to be celebrated at the cathedral in Cuernavaca. The purpose of my sermon would be to initiate a project making the Bible the focus in his diocese.

Before accepting his offer, I took some time to be alone and pray. I even asked one of the priests at my sister's church near the university to speak with me. The priest and I noted that the bishop's invitation showed the Catholic Church in Latin America was opening to a more inclusive approach regarding the Bible. I told him I wanted to be a part of this forward movement. This invitation could be an opportunity to build a bridge between Protestants and Catholics. Then we spoke about Calvin's statement in his *Institutes*, "Scandal in the Church No Occasion for Leaving It," in which Calvin said he would cross ten seas for the sake of Christian unity.[59] Surely if one of the founders of our church, a leader of the Protestant Reformation, had taken this stand, how could it be wrong for me to accept this invitation from the bishop? So I said yes, thinking that nothing could be more consistent with my Christian faith than to join the bishop in a project Calvin would have encouraged.[60]

My students were constantly asking me why Presbyterians looked down on Catholics. In November 1963, I saw an opportunity. I managed to have the seniors invited to observe a Mass in Spanish at El Altillo, a nearby Roman Catholic seminary. Following the Mass, our hosts served us breakfast with a seating arrangement that allowed for maximum personal mixing. In a spirit of shy camaraderie, there emerged tentative questions about each other's tradition, but also simple conversations. As we were leaving, we promised to pray for one another. When we got back, one of my students blurted out with conviction, which clearly spoke for the rest, "I am troubled but happy. They are Christians, but we don't treat them as such."[61]

This is what I hoped would happen; my students had begun to open their hearts to Catholics. Soon after we attended the Mass at

El Altillo, one of my friends at my seminary warned me to be more careful. He told me our visit might have negative repercussions for my job. I felt hemmed in. It was problematic for me to take students to see secular plays, even to visit the nearby Catholic seminary, or to meet with a Catholic bishop. The narrow-mindedness of the seminary officials was difficult to tolerate.

As I was pondering, I caught myself. While I criticized seminary leaders for their narrow-mindedness, I realized I myself was also being critical. They had not grown up in a Catholic family, as I had. They had not studied in American seminaries where there was more openness than in Mexico. They had not wrestled for years to develop a synthesis of Catholic and Protestant views. I so wanted to be more tolerant, but just as it was not easy for me, it was also hard for them.

While wrestling within, I reflected on the history between Catholics and Protestants in Mexico. In the early days, Protestants had been targeted by the Catholic Church. In fact, in 1875 Catholic zealots had massacred members of a new Protestant congregation. The massacre is called *Mártires de Acapulco* (Martyrs of Acapulco).[62] Even though this had happened more than eighty-eight years before, I could understand why it was hard for the president of the seminary and other conservative Protestants to forget. Recalling this horrible event helped me understand their animosity. But did it make sense to allow the ripple effect of horrible events like this to blemish all Catholics for so many years?

Every professor in our seminary was expected to teach theology in conformity with the Westminster Confession of Faith, drafted by English and Scottish theologians between 1643 and 1647. The fact that it was such an extremely anti-Roman document led to conflict among the faculty. It spoke of the Roman

Catholic Church as an apostate body, led not by Christ but by the "Antichrist," the pope. This document had become the doctrinal standard of the National Presbyterian Church of Mexico.

I focused on the essential unity of the one church of Jesus Christ and refused to teach any form of anti-Catholicism. In a seminary faculty meeting held in mid-November 1963, I proposed a compromise in which I indicated that neither Luther nor Calvin had gone as far as the Westminster Assembly of the Divines. I pointed out that by 1903, English-speaking Presbyterians around the globe had revised the Confession by removing most of the offensive language used to describe the pope and the Church of Rome from the original text. I suggested we do the same. Then, in a larger meeting including faculty and students held the following week, my students found this proposal reasonable, but the president did not.

By late November, it became clear to me that the seminary president and I saw things very differently. While bringing harmony to relations between Protestants and Catholics was at the heart of my work, the president preferred the anti-Catholic status quo. Though others supported my efforts to found the Association of Theological Seminaries and Bible Schools, the president remained silent each time the topic was mentioned in faculty meetings. My conflict with the president was obvious. Early one evening as I was leaving class, a colleague whispered, "Either you are with us or against us." Also, I had noticed that Ruth's father had become more distant and more critical of me than usual.

My worst fear was to be accused of heresy. I considered how I could avoid that. Could I promise to never attend more meetings with Catholic leaders, to never accept invitations to Catholic events with my students, and to take an anti-Catholic stance in my teaching according to the Westminster Confession of Faith? Then

MY DIVIDED HEART

I remembered Tex-Mex and my experience baptizing the young prisoners at the Kleberg County Jail. Back then, I had chosen to follow my heart and to do what I believed to be right. I thought of Luther and Calvin, who had risked their lives to speak out against what they thought was wrong. If I backed down, I might not be able to forgive myself.

That spring, I received a phone call from Marina, my stepmother, in Los Mochis, Sinaloa, saying that my father was dying. Seventeen years had passed since I had last seen him and Marina. Even though it was hard for me to leave the seminary, I decided to go to Los Mochis to be with Papá and Marina. I looked forward to seeing Marina and hoped for a meaningful connection with Papá. He was in so much pain that he could hardly speak. I was sorry not to see Magaly, who was away with friends. However, I was able to tell Marina once again how much I appreciated the fact that she had paid my tuition for Tex-Mex that first year. She was glad to have played a part in my accomplishments. I was by his deathbed one whole week. Finally, I had to leave. I felt sad to say goodbye knowing I would probably never see any of them again. Marina called soon after to say my father had died.[63]

During my return trip, I thought about Papá and wondered if he, while facing the challenge of dying, felt lonely as I did. I wished we could have openly talked about our feelings. I too was facing a challenge—the biggest challenge of my life—one that could impact both my career and my family. I kept debating whether I should be true to my heart or dissemble my feelings to placate the seminary president. After my return, I had little time to ponder this dilemma.

Early one morning in mid-May 1964, my office telephone rang. It was the president. By the tone of his voice, I could tell he was angry. Without saying hello, he told me to appear in two days at Príncipe de Paz Presbyterian Church at ten in the morning. I would meet with him and some members of the National Presbyterian Church of Mexico. It was so ironic—Príncipe *de Paz* (Prince of Peace), not only the name but the place. This had been our church in Mexico City, the church where Ruth and I had married eleven years before.

That afternoon, I got in touch with a friend of mine who served on the board of the National Presbyterian Church of Mexico. I asked him to please tell me what was happening. He hesitated to speak freely but intimated I might be tried for heresy. Apparently the president, together with some highly placed church officials, did intend to charge me with heresy. I tried to stay calm. No one was truly backing me up. Unfortunately, even my wife was embarrassed by my position. She was afraid we would have to leave Mexico and that I would have no way of supporting the family.

My mind raced ahead. What if they actually proved me guilty? That could damage my reputation in the Presbyterian Church worldwide. It might even end my career. Ruth and her father might never forgive me. My hands started to tremble and my head ached. Although I did not want to learn more bad news, I decided it was important to be better informed so I got in touch with another friend from the board of the National Presbyterian Church. From him I gathered I would be brought before the jurisdiction in which the seminary was located, Mexico City. This was not a controversy with my faculty colleagues, as such. It was a controversy within the Presbyterian Church as a whole. I also learned that the president of my seminary had talked to some highly placed church officials concerning what he alleged were heresies that I was teaching at the seminary.[64]

As I learned more, I became convinced it would be hard for me to continue as dean of the seminary. This motivated me to phone one of my colleagues at the Austin Presbyterian Theological Seminary. I told him I might lose my job or, even worse, be charged with heresy. My colleague promised to tell the seminary president what was happening.

When I got home the following evening, I found Jorge Luis was still awake. Though he was only eight, he was more tuned in to me than most people. While he did not know the details, he understood I was facing a big challenge. When he asked me what was happening, I told him I was having a hard time, and he offered to pray with me. We prayed together that our whole family, and both of our churches—Aunt Cachuy's church over by the university and our church Príncipe de Paz—might be blessed with the "peace of Christ."

Then Jorge Luis asked what "peace of Christ" meant. I pondered for a minute then spoke about the time Jesus was being interrogated by Pilate before he was crucified. Pilate asked Jesus if he was the King of the Jews. I told Jorge Luis that Pilate's accusatory way of questioning Jesus could have easily put Jesus on the defensive or made him angry. At that moment, Jesus knew, everyone knew, that his life was at stake. Instead of being infuriated or submissive, Jesus answered surprisingly, "You say so."[65] I told Jorge Luis I wanted to have that kind of inner peace too.

I was delighted when Jorge Luis said he remembered when I told that story in church just before Easter. He said it scared him, because he knew the whole time what was going to happen to Jesus. He confessed it also made him want to be like Jesus, when he is faced with something really hard.

After spending that peaceful time with my son, I felt easier about the forthcoming meeting with the president and others at Príncipe de Paz Church the next day. My time with Jorge Luis also helped me sleep better that night.

The next morning I arrived at 9:59 a.m. The president and the "highly placed officials" had already taken their places. The president sat at one end of the long table and told me to seat myself at the other end. Then he listed my offenses. Heresy number one: I taught falsely that the Catholic Church was a Christian church. Heresy number two: I demeaned the clergy of the Presbyterian Church by teaching (valuing) to an exaggerated degree the equality of laypeople. Heresy number three: I took students to see plays like *Gideon* or *A Man for All Seasons*, while other professors took students to theatrical performances featuring only biblical characters.[66]

I never dreamt they would go to this extreme. Even though I knew they believed that Catholics were doomed to hell and damnation, I felt this was preposterous. How could I respect people who honestly felt that way? Of course, I knew Catholics were Christians, not less than Presbyterians.

Though I respected the president and the board, I refused to bow to them. Rather than meekly accepting their position, I decided to follow my conscience and speak the truth, as Luther had done in the sixteenth century. They recalled, almost angrily, that I had preached from the pulpit of the cathedral in Cuernavaca, and that I had disregarded their belief that Catholics were doomed to hell. I told them that in my view, Catholics were also Christians, not of any lesser standing before God than Presbyterians.

I used the works of John Calvin and Martin Luther, the leaders of the Protestant Reformation, to show they were not

MY DIVIDED HEART

anti-Catholic. First and foremost, they were adamant reformers who hoped to make changes in the Catholic church, not leave it. Since I was a layperson, how could I possibly agree with the president and church officials that the laity should be disempowered? Once again, I looked to our Protestant forefathers to help in my defense: Luther and Calvin placed supreme importance on the Bible and the laity. Luther and Calvin both believed the priesthood was not a segregated class of religious officials but part of a community made up of all believers.

Regarding the third heresy, I said that it seemed irrational to forbid seminary students from seeing plays about anything other than biblical characters. Shouldn't the purpose of seminary be to prepare students not only to preach but to understand human relationships in their contemporary lives? What better way to open their hearts and minds to human struggles than through contemporary literature, in addition to studying the Bible? Furthermore, I used examples from the Bible to show that people in the Bible were far from pure.

I defended myself with the Bible in one hand and the works of Calvin and Luther in the other. I said, "You may judge me as heretical but I will not relinquish my commitment to Luther, Calvin, and the Bible."[67] After I made this statement, the group asked me to leave the room to give them time for deliberation. After an hour, they called me back. To my surprise, and the chagrin of my accusers, I was found innocent. I was pleased and embarrassed when my students rose up to applaud the verdict.[68] Because the officials had accepted the theological conclusions of Luther and Calvin, I was exonerated.

I was gratified when those who had attended the trial complimented me. Of course, I wondered what had led to my exoneration.

Perhaps the group had predetermined I would be overwhelmed by the Presbyterian leaders and was taken aback when I stood up for myself. Maybe they thought they had an airtight case against me and did not expect me to speak up. Later I learned the seminary president saw that Luther's and Calvin's positions supported my stands on the importance of the laity and inclusivity of Catholics. I was exonerated based on my knowledge of Luther's and Calvin's teachings. My accusers may have recognized that, in all likelihood, I knew more in this particular area of theology than they did. I dared to believe no one in that group wanted to find themselves in a debate with me, nor did I want to debate them. While saddened to have seen such a show of pharisaic self-righteousness in the leaders of my own church, I was relieved.

Yet my exoneration did not end the matter. I knew I would soon need to decide whether to hide my real beliefs and pretend penitence or to continue to stand up for what I believed, even if it meant losing my position at the seminary. My absolution would not put an end to the hostility from the seminary and churches in Mexico. The trial showed, in fact, that I would most likely not be able to survive in the midst of so much enmity and suspicion.

What more could I do? I decided to invite my students and faculty colleagues to a meeting with the seminary president. I wanted them to witness the situation with their own eyes and ears. At the meeting, I asked the president what future might there be for me at the seminary? "Will there be another time that you would take me before ecclesiastical authorities with another charge instead of coming to me as a brother and a friend and expressing your concern?" When I posed this question to the president, he would not answer.

My colleagues, in one voice, demanded, "Sir, you have heard the question. Answer it."

Then the president said to me, "Clergy does not address laity." They told him that was not a sufficient answer. That was what I was afraid of, so I reached into my pocket and brought out my letter of resignation.[69]

The president's statement made in the company of my faculty and students was an insult not only to me, a member of the laity, but to the seminary students as well. When I first came to the seminary, I had explained to the president why I had chosen not to be ordained. He said he understood. Now, however, he was refusing to answer me and my colleagues because I was a member of the laity.

My heart was racing. I was breathing hard. What must have been a total of ten minutes felt like an hour. Now, seventeen years since the incident in the South Texas café, I was experiencing another form of discrimination, this time from my seminary president. If I, as the seminary dean, could be treated this way in cosmopolitan Mexico City, what might be happening to laypeople in congregations all over Mexico? The president's position was unconscionable.

The mitigating aspect of this whole experience was my students. Every student save one declared, "If Professor Lara-Braud leaves, we leave with him."[70] Even so, I stood up for the dissenter. As one of my students later recalled:

> As a fellow human being and a Christian, Jorge stood up for the lone dissenter, asking respect for his point of view. However, he was disappointed when most of his students ostracized the dissenter nevertheless.[71]

My dream of serving as dean of the seminary in Mexico had ended. This was tough in another way as well. I had wanted to be a creative bridge between Protestants and Catholics in Mexico, and for that matter, in the Spanish-speaking world, and it seemed that dream too was ending. More serious and sad was the attitude of my in-laws and my wife, who sided with the accusers—not publicly, but behind the scenes. My in-laws wondered why I had to teach those things and why I couldn't just teach the Bible.[72]

Now, looking back, I can understand how hard this was for Ruth. Since she and her family were prominent members of the Presbyterian Church, the church was of ultimate importance to her. My trial not only had jeopardized her relationship with her church, Príncipe de Paz, but it had hurt her family. This struggle had been so all-consuming that I had failed to be empathetic.

My next big challenge was to communicate with her father, Señor Marroquín. I had attempted to build warmer relations by undertaking translation work for the American Bible Society, his employer. Though our relationship was not on solid ground, I hoped he would be supportive when the chips were down.

That, however, was not the case. At our first meeting after the trial, he met me with a barrage of criticism. I felt disappointed that he so strongly disagreed with the outcome of the trial. I wondered if he had spoken to the seminary president, since he was echoing his views almost exactly.

He asked me why I wasn't more concerned about the spiritual future of my birth family. So long as they remained Catholics, he thought, there was no hope for them.[73]

At that moment, I remembered my first year at Tex-Mex, when my Catholic roots influenced me so much. I felt those roots holding me so strongly that I was unable to relax and to feel at home at Tex-Mex. Then, a year later, I saw my way forward—not *either/or*, but *both/and*. What was obvious to me now—a synthesis of Catholicism and Protestantism—was not obvious then. So why should it be so for him?

Of course, I wondered how a professed Christian could condemn a whole group of people, especially people in his own son-in-law's family, simply because they had a different religious affiliation. The Bible teaches us to love our neighbor, as exemplified in the Parable of the Good Samaritan. If Señor Marroquín were to take biblical teachings literally, as he himself suggested, how could it possibly be right to discount one's Catholic brothers and sisters?

Clearly, Señor Marroquín was embarrassed by my stand and frustrated that he could not persuade me to change. Obviously, I was asking him to choose between his daughter's husband and his church. In addition, he was angry at me for betraying his trust. He had recommended me for the deanship, and this was the result. My actions challenged his religion to its core—his view of heaven and earth, his faith in and understanding of God—which he was committed to defend at all costs. There was no room in his mind or heart for my approach. To me, his stand seemed closed-minded, but for me to condemn him and his family would be to dismiss their long-held beliefs as unimportant. So, I prayed to God to open my heart and to accept them as they were.

This conversation with Señor Marroquín reinforced my determination to strive for unity. Even though my old dream had burst, my experience with conflicts stemming from my work as dean strengthened my resolve to become an imaginative ambassador between diverse parts of the church. I wished our Presbyterian

Church could be more open to diverse views and faiths, as the Catholic Church was beginning to be.

I looked longingly upon the changes taking place in my "old Catholic Church," which was becoming more inclusive. It was 1964. Pope John XXIII was a saintly pastor of peasant origins.[74] He had convened the Second Vatican Council on October 11, 1962, informally known as Vatican II. Winds of church renewal were blowing. The Bible was being made available to everyone in their own language. Laity would be permitted to have closer relationships with clergy and to fulfill important jobs in their churches. Most dear to my heart, the Catholic Church would encourage ecumenical projects around the world and would respect Protestants and Jews in new ways. While the Presbyterians in Mexico were still listening to voices of fear, Catholics were opening up in ways that were heartening to me and so many others as well. While I hated to admit it, I was feeling more comfortable with the Catholic Church than my own.

Two days after the heresy trial, President David Stitt invited me to serve as assistant professor of missions at the Austin Presbyterian Theological Seminary. Dr. Stitt agreed to give me twenty-four hours to consider the offer. Because accepting it would represent a significant turning point for our whole family, Ruth and I prayed and talked it over. Finally, she reluctantly agreed the only positive way forward for our family would be to return to Austin. The following day, I called President Stitt to tell him I would accept his invitation.

CHAPTER NINE

Opening People's Hearts

*Our enemies may kill us,
the visionaries,
but they can't kill our visions.*

—Jorge Lara-Braud, "Mi Jornada"

In mid-June 1964, I went to Austin to find a house for us. Ruth and Jorgito came in early July. Of course, we were sad to leave our families in Mexico City. Having been dean for only two years, the abrupt end of my dream was devastating to me. As a result, the United States would become our new home. However, I had to remember the United States was not our country. Neither Ruth nor I were even citizens. I had only a green card. When I returned to Austin, I became concerned that the United States had only sporadically lived up to its ideal of inclusiveness as stated in the Pledge of Allegiance: "one nation under God, indivisible, with liberty and justice for all."

My hope was for every single person in the United States to be treated with respect, as I had been at Tex-Mex, Austin College, and Austin Presbyterian and Princeton seminaries. I was aware, however, that so long as there existed a great division between Protestants and Catholics, the United States would not live up to its stated ideals. Protestants were often prejudiced against Hispanics, who were generally Catholic.

Although I was distraught by the events that had so recently occurred in Mexico, I did not anticipate the publicity that my heresy trial would generate. Invitations began to come to me from faraway places like Geneva, New York, Buenos Aires, and other Latin American capitals. The bishop of Cuernavaca, who was to be one of the more influential voices at Vatican II, had commended me to a number of reform-minded Roman Catholic bishops and to a new group of theologians who were to be the founders of the movement known as liberation theology. Though the trial caused me heartache at the time, it propelled me toward a far more fruitful calling than I would have experienced had I remained at the seminary in Mexico.

Even John Mackay, the president of Princeton Seminary, was rooting for me from afar during my struggle at the heresy trial. Because we shared a common vision of Christian unity, he recommended me to the Presbyterian leaders who were selecting a delegation for the Nineteenth General Council of Reformed Churches to be held in Frankfurt, Germany, in August 1964. I eagerly accepted the invitation to serve as a consultant at the conference.

The theme of the conference was "Come, Creator Spirit! For the Calling of the Churches Together." As I listened to the Presbyterian Taiwanese scholar C. H. Hwang's presentation, I felt heartened. The emphasis was on religious unity—Protestant, Jew, and Catholic—and the unity of nations.[75]

Being in Frankfurt that summer regenerated me. What a contrast to the fear and reprisals I had so recently encountered in Mexico. Presbyterians from around the world were searching for ways to bring together Protestants and Catholics. Many at the conference were praising the late Pope John XXIII and talking about the upcoming "Roman Catholic Ecumenical Council Vatican II," which would take place in Rome that November.

While we were in Frankfurt, John Mackay and I began to talk directly about the need for bilingual graduate theological programs for the growing Hispanic population in the United States. We wanted to empower and educate Hispanic leaders. Our hope was to stage conferences focusing on the role of the church in raising the living standards of Hispanics in the States.

I returned from Frankfurt in time to prepare for classes in September. In one of my courses, The Ecumenical Movement, I focused on a historical survey of the quest for Christian unity with special reference to the World Council of Churches and the current Protestant–Roman Catholic ecumenical dialogue. I talked about some of my own experiences, particularly what happened after I responded positively to Bishop Méndez Arceo's invitations to visit with him at the Catholic cathedral in Cuernavaca. Students were amazed to hear of a heresy trial in the twentieth century. None of them knew that the struggle for even minimum dialogue between Catholics and Protestants in Latin America could be so difficult.

At lunches in the seminary cafeteria, we would discuss how the lack of inclusiveness was at odds with "the American Dream." Most of the students had never directly faced any form of discrimination. It had not occurred to them that the American Dream didn't include someone like me whose skin was the color of maple syrup.

In the spring of 1965, leaders in the U.S. Presbyterian Church were establishing the Hispanic-American Institute (hereafter, the Institute). Sponsored by the Northern and Southern branches of the Presbyterian Church, the Institute's headquarters would be located at the Austin Presbyterian Theological Seminary. Church leaders appointed a board of directors and invited me to be the executive director.

After learning that John Mackay would be the official consultant to the Institute, I agreed to serve. He knew how to move within the various church institutions of the United States and had the prestige essential for starting up this new venture. He was invaluable to me as an older brother, elder statesman, and gospel prophet.[76]

Right away, John Mackay introduced me to his friend John Sinclair, who became the chair of the Institute's board. Having served on the Presbyterian Commission on Ecumenical Mission and Relations, he had the right experience for our kind of work.

Left to right: John Sinclair, Dr. John Mackay, and Jorge, 1968

We were delighted when other Austin-area academic and religious institutions, such as the Episcopal Seminary of the Southwest and the Institute of Latin American Studies at the University of Texas, became partners with the Hispanic-American Institute. Later the United Methodist Church, the Episcopal Church, the Disciples of Christ, Lutherans (Missouri Synod, Lutheran Church in America, and American Lutheran Church), and finally, Roman Catholics through the National Association of Hispanic Priests, known by the acronym PADRES (*Padres Asociados para Derechos*

Religiosos Educationales y Sociales), became affiliated with the Institute.

At the Institute, we all realized an important way to open people's hearts would be through firsthand experiences. This realization motivated us to plan the January Seminars. They began in 1967 with one week of study at the Austin Presbyterian Theological Seminary. This was followed by two weeks in the field visiting church and political leaders, as well as Hispanic groups in South Texas. The group would then return to Austin for a week of study and reflection. The focus was on Mexican and Mexican American history, culture, and language. Students and professors as well as governmental, church, and political leaders from across the United States participated.

The following fall we were asked to design a similar program at Princeton Theological Seminary for pastors in the New York metropolitan area. These seminars served as pilot programs that soon spread to other areas of the country. Participants said that these direct experiences exposing the struggles of Hispanics opened their hearts. The seminars represented the type of work we had originally envisioned for the Institute, a think tank above the fray of politics.

Soon after I established the groundwork for the Institute and the seminars, Austin College asked me to give its commencement address. In recognition of my accomplishments, my alma mater awarded me an honorary doctorate. In that address on August 25, 1967, I spelled out my commitment to encourage Americans to live up to the ideals stated in the Declaration of Independence.[77] I referred to the patriots of 1776 as God's coworkers in the creation of a truly new and humane society in which all people, simply on account of their humanity, are to be treated as equals before heaven and earth. So long as any portion of the citizenry is deprived of its participation in the decision-making process, the whole of the new creation stands under the shadow of self-contradiction and eventual self-destruction. I told the audience because the United States was the focus of those aspiring to freedom around the world, it was essential for the nation to live up to its stated ideals.[78]

Ruth, Jorge, and Jorge Luis at Austin College in Sherman, Texas, August 1967

My address made me more receptive to representatives from La Raza Unida (The United Race) when they approached the Institute. At that time, La Raza was a somewhat radical and fairly loose community of two or three hundred social, political, and cultural groups from Texas and Southern California, staffed mostly by idealistic volunteers from the Catholic Church.[79] La Raza asked us to help plan and execute its winter conference scheduled for the following year in San Antonio. Although we at the Institute were in accord with La Raza's goals to campaign for better housing, work, and educational opportunities for Hispanics, we were wary of its members' operating style. While they led boycotts and sit-ins, our way had been to work quietly through diplomacy and conversations.

La Raza's challenging invitation moved us to reassess our situation. Yes, we had been coasting along believing we were making progress even though little had been happening. Yes, highly respected Anglo Protestants like John Mackay and John Sinclair had dedicated themselves completely to the cause espoused by the Institute. However, while the major Anglo denominations had committed financially to the Institute, many Protestant church members hesitated to reach out to Hispanics in meaningful ways and include them in their lives. Protestants and Catholics lived in separate neighborhoods and rarely communicated with one another. Because most Hispanics were Catholics, and the majority of Anglos were Protestants, forging links between those two groups was integral to our work as peacemakers. While we had made token changes, the walls of division remained strong. Changing the status quo would be difficult, not only for conservatives but for me personally.

I admit, part of me also wanted to coast along with the veneer of peace, as it was the easiest path. I tried to be detached as I considered what would be best for the Hispanic people who were at the heart of our mission. But how could I be neutral? I was Mexican. How could we remain true to our ideals without alienating our funders and conservative supporters?

To break through the walls dividing Hispanics and Anglos, we needed to take aggressive action. With a growing awareness of problems facing Hispanic Americans like discrimination in schools, limited job opportunities, and meager political representation, we felt compelled to partner with La Raza. We hoped that working together would empower both groups.

My struggle was similar to that of other Mexican Americans. But it was also different. I had an advanced education and was teaching at a prominent seminary. However, like them, I often felt quietly, and not so quietly, put down. Deep inside, I knew how awful it feels to be treated poorly. Each time I went home to Mexico to visit my family, I noticed that even in my home country, Anglo Americans were more accepted than I was.

In 1963, while still dean in Mexico City, I had been invited to speak at the Montreat World Mission Conference in North Carolina. In my address, I said I was "semicolored." I was not white; neither was I "Negro"; I was in-between. Even if I temporarily had forgotten about this, there were some members within my own church who would not only remind me that I was not white but communicate that in some way, somehow, I was not nearly as good as they were.[80]

Remembering how awful I felt about being discriminated against helped me clarify my position. All around us, the civil rights movement was exploding. How could I or the Hispanic-American Institute stand safely on the sidelines? After reaching a decision myself, I spoke with the Institute's board. Together, we agreed to risk losing some support in order to work with La Raza Unida.

Throughout November and December 1967, the Institute worked with La Raza representatives to lay the groundwork for their conference scheduled to take place at John F. Kennedy High School in San Antonio on January 6, 1968. La Raza invited me to be the keynote speaker. I accepted with apprehension. At this conference, La Raza made a declaration representing 1,200 Hispanics that stated:

> We point to the disproportionate number of Mexican-American casualties in Vietnam, roughly twice in comparison to their population percentage in the Southwest, and recall that Mexican-Americans were awarded a greater proportional number of decorations than any other ethnic group from this country during the Second World War.[81]

It horrified me to see how Hispanic American veterans were expected to give their lives for their country, but then were treated abysmally when they returned from war. If life is precious enough to be sacrificed in war, it is precious enough to be respected in peace.[82] Time and again, in speeches and to the press, I stated: "Veterans challenged, in and out of court, the blatant legacy of discrimination still prevalent in the Southwest, often displayed by glaring signs or the brutal words 'No Mexicans allowed.'"[83] I reiterated in many speeches that Mexican Americans were the "forgotten minority," and that the time had come for Mexican Americans to have a share of public power. They were on approximately the same level as African Americans in terms of their lack of employment, low salaries, dilapidated housing, and limited political representation and voice.

Not surprisingly, as we reached out to help groups of Hispanics, the more traditionalist members of our board grew increasingly unhappy with our work. These people argued that our job was to keep the peace. I disagreed. We needed not only to keep the peace, but to make peace. To accomplish this we needed to ensure every person had equal opportunities. The opposition continued to charge that, like Dr. King's followers, we were "stirring up trouble." Similar to a poker player, I tried to take a cautious position, not always showing my cards.

In February 1968, I wrote to John Sinclair explaining my dilemma. In my letter, I told him I hoped he had received La Raza's statement concerning the boycott against Humble Oil and Refining Company. I added that I considered it somewhat unfortunate that the Associated Press release, which was appearing in many newspapers throughout the country, associated only one person's name with this boycott—my own.[84]

I knew this situation would upset our more right-wing supporters. And I was not wrong. That April, I received a critical letter from Sherwood Reisner, the headmaster of my alma mater, Presbyterian Pan American School, and board member of the Institute. He declared:

> I have been disappointed by your naïve support of this front group. La Raza Unida has already done some real damage in Kingsville, and perhaps in other areas. It has only a limited appeal to a fringe group. The native Texan is still not ready for the ministration of the carpet-bagger.[85]

Reisner informed me that a number of his financial supporters vowed they would no longer donate to Tex-Mex if it continued to turn out "rabble-rousers." It seemed they felt their livelihood was threatened by strikes and boycotts led by La Raza and encouraged by people like me. People like Reisner were in favor of Mexican Americans having equal opportunities, in theory. In actuality, for them, tranquility trumped human rights.

Sherwood Reisner, president of the Presbyterian Pan American School (Tex-Mex) from 1956 to 1980[86]

This is partly why Reisner then devised a plan to oust me from the directorship of the Institute. Without warning me, prior to our October 1968 board meeting, he contacted all the members of the board except me, urging them to join him in forcing my resignation. Reisner had not taken into account his father-in-law, John Mackay. When Mackay learned of Reisner's plan, he compelled Reisner himself to resign from the board. That December, Reisner wrote to tell me that the Tex-Mex board of trustees had voted to discontinue their affiliation with the Institute. This event was challenging for the Institute's board, but it was even more so for me because I still felt allegiance to my school. Time and again during this period I felt grateful for John Mackay's support.

While we lamented these conflicts with the conservatives, we realized our focus should be on changing the status of Hispanic people as the "forgotten minority." Powerlessness had become rooted in their lifestyle years ago when they came here to work in the fields. Unable to speak or understand English, they found their means of survival depended on their meek acceptance of an inferior status.[87] Realization of this fact led us to focus on empowerment through language. This became a central focus of our work. Consequently, I made a presentation to the National Council of Churches (NCC) in February 1968, explaining the need for an office of Spanish-American Ministries. The NCC established it that same year, and that gave us greater legitimacy as we worked to develop bilingual programs in schools and Hispanic ministries in churches throughout the United States.

As had happened to me time and again in life, I then met a person who fueled our movement forward—Father Patrick Flores. Patrick, the son of migrant laborers, had made it his life's work to stand together with the poor Mexican American workers in South Texas. Father Flores was appointed in 1970 as the first Hispanic American bishop in the United States. He is the one who introduced me to the leaders of PADRES, headquartered in San Antonio.[88] PADRES was a dedicated group of around 350 priests who focused on assisting the most impoverished men, women, and children in the Hispanic American community.

Through PADRES, I came to know Father Edmundo Rodriguez of Our Lady of Guadalupe Church in San Antonio, who also served on the board of the Institute. From us he learned about our focus on police brutality against minorities. Hence, it was not surprising when he called in November 1971 asking me to help PADRES find creative ways to deal with similar problems in San

Antonio. I was disheartened to learn that in the past ten months, ten young Hispanic men had been killed by the police—many of them shot in the back. He said unless something was done, San Antonio might explode.

We planned a march that would end at the Alamo, inviting the entire police force and concerned citizens to attend. PADRES sponsors and the police chief of San Antonio worked out the details. The San Antonio City Council set a date for Saturday, November 20, 1971.

As I drove to San Antonio that Saturday, I was wondering how I could connect with the San Antonio police. So far, no one else had made that connection. Then I had an idea. I would point out that many of the Hispanic names memorialized on the Alamo walls, names like Jiménez and Fuentes, were listed alongside the well-known heroes, like Bowie and Travis. Those Hispanics had died together with other Texans defending the Alamo in 1836. Just as they stood and fought together, so should we stand and fight for and with one another.

When I first arrived, Father Rodriguez and others dressed me in a priest's robe so that my remarks to the policemen would carry more authority. The march participants included Catholic and Protestant clergy members, college students, attorneys, labor leaders, and family members of the victims of police brutality—around 1,200 people.

All went smoothly until we passed the county jail and saw two officers roughing up a young Mexican American in handcuffs. Some of the marchers, seething with anger, surged toward the police. Father Edmundo and others held them back. As leaders of the march, we were anxious lest this dangerous moment explode into a riot like ones that had occurred in other major U.S. cities.

But thanks to the monitors and the careful organization that had preceded the march, we avoided an explosion.

As I was pointing out the Hispanic names on the Alamo walls at the end of the march, I got fired up. I shook my finger at the crowd and said, "Some day I will tell my son about this march." Seeing the startled faces of the crowd, it dawned on me—they thought I was a Catholic priest! While the idea of dressing me in a priest's robe had been for a good cause, I felt it had been duplicitous and resolved not to do such a thing again.

The march had a positive effect. Officers singled out for their violent behavior were taken off the street and placed on desk duty. With the help of PADRES, peace was reinstated.

By the 1970s, there had been moments when the struggle had been so difficult that I wanted to give up—we all did! However, we were encouraged by people like John Mackay, John Sinclair, and Bishop Flores not to lose heart. During times like our march to the Alamo, our faith in the positive effects of our work was restored.

The deeper I found myself involved in the struggle of Mexican Americans, the more clearly I understood the gospel. It was truly a joy to be able to speak to hundreds of impoverished people in so many places. Knowing the liberation that comes from viewing these realities through the prism of faith, then speaking from that perspective, was wonderful. As a theologian, I searched for ways Christian faith could address people suffering unjustly. Often, I was stopped by people who would say that things never change—no water, no education, no rights...

I would reply, "Yes, except for one thing. We are no longer hopeless. We have seen the vision of the kingdom of God, the vision of the reign of justice and peace and love." Then I would add,

"Our enemies may kill us, the visionaries, but they can't kill our visions."[89]

During my five years at the Institute, we had labored together to build bridges between Hispanics and Anglos. Our goal was to reflect on the Pledge of Allegiance: "One nation under God, indivisible, with liberty and justice for all." Though still far from realizing our dream, where this nation could become a place in which every single person would be treated with respect, we had made some positive steps forward. In addition to our work in developing bilingual programs in schools and churches in Texas and beyond, we also helped to form a whole new generation of Hispanic leaders. Our most positive contribution was invisible. Like the vision of God's kingdom, it represented the open hearts of both Hispanics and Anglos.

CHAPTER TEN

Anguish and Achievement

*My grace is sufficient for you,
for power is perfected in weakness.*
—2 Corinthians 12:9 (IB)

From 1964 to 1969, while my career was blossoming, my marriage was deteriorating. Almost from the beginning of our relationship, Ruth and I had struggled. In high school, I had fallen in love not only with Ruth but also with her family. Because I had lost my sense of family and security when my parents separated, and again when I left home, I longed to belong to a real family again.

Ruth and I fell into a vicious circle. Anytime there was difficulty, Ruth sought support from her father while I ignored the problem and threw myself into my work. By doing so the chasm of resentment between us deepened. Finally, we both recognized the marriage was in jeopardy. Desperate to save our marriage, I had allowed Ruth and her father to persuade me to prematurely leave my doctoral work at Princeton and accept the deanship of the seminary in Mexico City. At first, I did not foresee the backlash of my own resentment for this decision. Later I realized what had transpired was as much my responsibility as it was Ruth's. I had failed to find a middle ground with Ruth and work things out together in a gracious and diplomatic way.

During the heresy trial, I felt that Ruth's allegiance to her birth family was stronger than her commitment to me. At the time of the trial, when I was engaged in one of the biggest challenges of my life, I felt she sided with her father. However, in hindsight, I realized that living through that trial was also agonizing for her. The Marroquíns were a highly respected Presbyterian family. No doubt, she was ashamed. Mexican families are often more interdependent and close-knit than families in the United States. The fact

I had been tried for heresy in her own family's church, Príncipe de Paz, was very hard for her. Although I tried to overlook that part of our life when I was serving as dean of the seminary in Mexico, it cast a shadow over our relationship from which we never recovered.

When we started our new life in the States, I kept hoping my resentment would subside; instead, it quietly festered for years. That is partly why I focused on my work more than my family. Part of the attraction of my work came from the ovations I received after speaking. While I was aware that no family could provide that kind of admiration on a constant basis, I still yearned for affirmation in my marriage.

While the distance between Ruth and me grew, I kept hoping our love for Jorge Luis would bring us closer. But Ruth's constant attention focused on Jorge Luis left little room for me to be close to him. Regardless, I still tried to be a good father, but to Ruth, and at times to my son, I did not measure up. Many fathers in Texas went hunting with their sons. Jorge Luis even saved money to buy a rifle, hoping I would take him hunting too. But I was no hunter. In fact, I had no use for guns.

On April 4, 1968, the moment I heard the news that Martin Luther King Jr. had been shot, I fell to my knees sobbing. For years, I had looked up to King as the person who most embodied Gandhi's ideal of nonviolence. Like King, I was also drawn to Gandhi's statements about the "transformative power of love." I too believed love could change oppressors into liberators. Losing that great man was like losing a dear friend.

Jorge Luis was only thirteen at the time and had never seen me cry. He stood beside me and watched silently. I could tell he wanted to comfort me, but he was not sure how to help. Then he did something that touched my heart. He brought his rifle to me and said, "Here, Dad. This might make you feel better. I promise never to shoot a rifle."[90] His compassion moved me. While I had so often wanted to reach out to him, that night he reached out to me.

After that, I looked for other ways we might become closer. He would often show me the reports and essays he wrote for school. I would praise his writing. "This is so elegant," I would say, as I made a circle with my thumb and forefinger to show my delight. I could tell by his face that he was also pleased.[91]

At the same time, he used to flip through my yellow writing tablets, admiring my penmanship and the care I took in preparing sermons and class lectures. He enjoyed attending chapel at the seminary and other churches when I was speaking or singing. Much later, he confided that listening to me made him proud. What he especially loved, he told me, was how I would say something on a high note toward the end of my sermon, then pause. For him, that was always a special moment.[92]

Though we never played basketball or baseball together, as I had hoped, I did teach him to drive in 1969. I used to encourage him to move into the driver's seat; then I would give him tips about how to look properly when backing out of the driveway.[93] I still treasure those times.

Sadly, I cut them short too soon. In the fall of 1969, I went into his makeshift darkroom to admire the photos he was developing. I knew that a breakup with Ruth was at hand and hoped to talk with Jorge Luis about my feelings, yet I felt awkward. I loved him but did not know how to tell him I was leaving; so I hesitated and left without speaking to him. He was young, only fourteen. I did not want to hurt him. Of course, I always regretted not talking to him that evening. What I did was much more hurtful to him than any conversation between us might have been.[94]

That very evening, I left my house and my family, thereby repeating what my father had done to us in Delicias. I felt ashamed. Yet, at the time there seemed to be no other option.

Again and again, I thought of that night when Jorge Luis brought me his rifle. Why, oh why, had I not reached out more lovingly to him? Why couldn't I have been like other fathers, who, in addition to working, took time to be with their children? Jorge Luis's dream to go hunting with me, I later realized, was more about being together than about killing animals.

Now I was devastated. I had failed both Jorge Luis and my wife. Even though I continued to send money to Ruth for Jorge Luis, it would take many years to overcome my guilt. Ruth and Jorge Luis joined her brother in Chile, then later returned to Mexico City.

During the following years, from 1970 to 1983, I entered into two more marriages that both ultimately failed.[95] It would have been much easier for me if my Mexican family had lived nearby. I was lonely and vulnerable. I so much wanted a home, warmth, and love that I often jumped too quickly.

How could things be so right with my career and in such shambles with my family? In Christian circles, the norm was for leaders, lay as well as ordained, once married, to remain faithful until death.

In 1972, John Mackay and John Sinclair suggested that I apply to become director of the Commission of Faith and Order of the National Council of Churches in New York City.[96] The commission was made up of fifty theologians and pastors representing thirty-three denominations including Orthodox, Roman Catholic, Protestant, and conservative evangelicals.

My task would be to lessen the divisions among these denominations. Simultaneously, I was also being considered to serve as an officer for the Commission of the World Council of Churches in Geneva. I felt delighted when I was told I was being chosen for these jobs because of my record as a "theologian in the trenches." This, no doubt, referred to my work with the Institute building bridges between Anglo Protestants and Hispanic Catholics. This wonderful opportunity to serve the church meant I would move to New York City. While I felt sad to leave my work as director of the Institute and seminary professor, I looked forward to this new chapter.

Jorge and Barbara Campbell, delegates of the Presbyterian Church in the U.S. at the Fifth Assembly of the World Council of Churches in Nairobi, December 1975

That December, when I arrived in New York City I began to wonder if an angel of destiny was hovering over me. Not only was

1972 the year I finally became a citizen of the United States, a country where I felt far more at home than in Mexico, but I was also asked to do the kind of work I loved, promoting unity. My official title would be executive director. James McCord, whom I had come to know and respect while I was studying at the Austin and Princeton seminaries, would act as the board chairman.

In August 1975, the Disciples of Christ denomination invited me to focus on my favorite topic—celebrating diversity—at their general assembly in San Antonio. As I contemplated my presentation, it occurred to me that there was no more appropriate place than the Southwest to speak about celebrating diversity. No other region encompasses such a wide mix of races, religions, languages, and national origins. I finished my speech by saying:

> I invite you tonight to join me in committing ourselves to a true celebration of our differences—black and white; brown, yellow, and red; male and female; Protestant, Catholic, Orthodox, Jew, and Muslim—in a community knit together, laboring and suffering together, keeping the unity of the spirit in the bond of peace. AMEN!"[97]

This statement encapsulated the focus of my work at the NCC. Little did I know then, I would soon become embroiled in a movement for social justice on an international scale.

Jorge addressing the 1975 National Workshop on Christian Unity.[98]

CHAPTER ELEVEN

Óscar Romero ¡Presente!

As a pastor, I am obliged by divine command to give my life for those whom I love—and that is for all Salvadorans, even for those who may assassinate me.

—Óscar Arnulfo Romero

B y 1977, the violence in El Salvador had escalated to such a degree that the National and World Councils of Churches were alerted. Consequently, they asked three representatives to go to El Salvador and witness the situation. The National Council of Churches sent Dr. Thomas Liggett, a top executive of the Christian Church (Disciples of Christ), along with Thomas Quigley, who was the director of the Office for Latin America of the National Conference of Catholic Bishops of the United States, and myself.[99]

Before my trip from New York to El Salvador, I researched Archbishop Óscar Romero and the struggle of the Salvadoran people. I learned that a majority of Salvadorans had been living in a state of conflict with wealthy landowners since the Spanish conquest in the sixteenth century. From 1870 to 1970, the largest landowners had succeeded in forcing the small farmers off their properties, and by 1971 the majority of the land was owned by the oligarchy. This wealthy group comprised approximately 4 percent of the population. People who depended on land for their livelihood had less than a subsistence plot or no land at all.[100]

For many years, Salvadorans had unsuccessfully tried nonviolent means to press their demands for land reform, a living wage, democracy, and education. Each time the people tried to speak out, wealthy landowners told them to wait until they died; then they would be blessed in heaven. Finally, a violent confrontation occurred in 1932. Peasants protested in the western part of the country, and the military responded by killing more than thirty thousand people in what Salvadorans still call "*La Matanza*" (the massacre).[101]

Mass grave of indigenous people killed during *La Matanza* in 1932[102]

In Central America, Mexico, Brazil, and other parts of Latin America, people despaired until they began to hear the hopeful notes of the Second Vatican Council (1962–65). Before Vatican II, the poor in El Salvador believed it was their duty to accept their plight. After Vatican II, the church shifted from an alignment with the wealthy few and the military to a focus on the poor. This shift by the church encouraged Salvadoran student groups and labor unions to organize and demand basic reforms.

This is the world into which Óscar Arnulfo Romero y Galdámes was born on August 15, 1917, in Ciudad Barrios, San Miguel Department, El Salvador. He attended local public school to grade three, the top grade at that time. Afterward, he was tutored until age thirteen, then left his home to attend the minor seminary in San Miguel, seven hours away by horseback.[103] In 1937, he went to the national seminary in San Salvador. While still there,

Romero's bishop sent him to Rome to complete his studies.[104] He was ordained in Rome in 1942.[105] After returning to El Salvador, he was assigned to San Miguel, where he served as the director of the ultraconservative archdiocesan newspaper *Orientación*.[106]

Óscar Arnulfo Romero as a boy[107]

Archbishop Romero's political beliefs could be partly explained by the fact that he grew up in San Miguel Department, a conservative region of the country. Indeed, it was largely because of his conservatism that the pope and other church leaders decided Romero was a safe choice to become the archbishop of San Salvador.[108] On February 23, 1977, only three months before Liggett, Quigley, and I went to El Salvador, he was appointed archbishop.[109] Until then, he had been an obscure country priest and bishop of a largely rural diocese. His consecration as archbishop had been received with pleasure by the armed forces and the fourteen families of the oligarchy who owned most of the land, the industries, the banks, and the transportation system. They considered him either an inoffensive nullity or an ally.[110]

When Óscar Romero took office, he stepped into a virtual time bomb of events that would profoundly alter the course of El Salvador's history. The fuse was lit on February 20, 1977, a mere three days before he was appointed. General Carlos Humberto Romero (no relation to the archbishop) was elected president after a blatantly fraudulent election in which the ruling "National Conciliation Party altered returns, filled ballot boxes with fraudulent votes and intimidated voters in the countryside to insure General Romero's victory."[111] Six days later, a mammoth event was staged in downtown San Salvador to protest the fraud. Closing off possible escape streets, soldiers fired their machine guns on the demonstrators. Estimates vary on the number of people killed, from single digits to hundreds. In the ensuing days, the true victor of the election, Colonel Ernesto Claramount, went into exile in Costa Rica, and the priests of the archdiocese began a prophetic denunciation of the electoral fraud and the massacre.[112]

A mere seventeen days after his appointment, everything changed for Archbishop Romero. His beloved friend, Father Rutilio Grande García, a sixteen-year-old boy, and an elderly man were ambushed and shot on March 12, 1977. They were traveling from Aguilares to Rutilio Grande's village of El Paisnal, where he was scheduled to say Mass at his church. Father Grande was killed not only for his denunciation of the massacre and election fraud, but also for teaching the Bible's preferential concern for the lowly and the landless.[113] His enemies denounced his teaching as unadulterated Marxism.

Archbishop Romero (front left) and
Father Grande (right)[114]

The killers proclaimed they would only give Father Grande's body to Archbishop Romero. He said that when he touched the bullet-riddled body of his friend, he felt he was touching the crucified body of Jesus. In silence he pledged to God that for the rest of his ministry he would follow the example of the martyred priest. And to the great consternation of generals and landlords who profess to be Christian, he did precisely that.

Father Grande had taught a group of Bible study leaders and had frequently shared with them the teachings of the Bible's bias for the poor. He was revered by his largely peasant parishioners. They were devastated when their spiritual leader and champion of their rights was assassinated. Because Father Grande was considered a subversive, merely possessing a Bible and a picture of him proved to be provocation enough for the military to kidnap and kill the possessor.[115]

The vehicle in which Father Grande was riding, after the ambush along the Aguilares road[116]

In the memorial Mass homily honoring Father Grande, Archbishop Romero demonstrated that he saw every person as an object of God's love. After denouncing the criminals with all of the rigor of an Old Testament prophet, Romero called them "brother assassins." Brothers? Yes, brothers, because neither God, nor the church, nor he had given up on them. He claimed those "brother assassins" were also made in the image of God; therefore, they must be treated as family members, no matter how wicked they had been.[117]

Soon after Father Grande's assassination, Romero specifically addressed his murder on the Catholic radio station YSAX. This was the beginning of a truly national pulpit and marked a turning point for Romero. From then on, practically every radio in the nation was tuned to YSAX for the Sunday morning Mass at the national cathedral. His on-air congregation included friend and foe alike and became the unofficial news source for information regarding assassinations, kidnappings, and disappearances.[118]

Archbishop Romero

Even though the U.S. government was aware of the shocking human rights abuses, including torture, murder, and imprisonment of innocent people, it continued to send money to support the Salvadoran military, because it feared the encroachment of communism throughout Central America.[119]

Soon after arriving in San Salvador in June of 1977, our team of three representatives met with the "Monseñor," a name Romero insisted we call him. At first, he seemed to be on guard. However, when I looked beneath his reserve, I found a simple, honest man, deeply interested in my work. He arrived together with two of his closest associates, who had recently been tortured. They were priests who now had swollen faces and twisted arms—signs of brutal beatings. Both spoke as if such torture was to be expected of anyone who told the truth. I asked them to explain to me what could have generated such animosity against both of them and the archbishop. One of the priests said:

> Our oligarchy considers itself Christian. That is why they seethe when they hear Monseñor Romero, the priests, the nuns, all of the catechists, denouncing their selfishness with biblical arguments, teachings of the pope, and citations from the bishops gathered in Medellín, Colombia, in 1968. That leaves them with no defense, so they resort to the worn-out strategy of calling "communism" everything that goes against their interests. The pity is that nothing is more effective when it comes to [gaining] the assistance of the United States for the oligarchies than to declare themselves threatened by communism.[120]

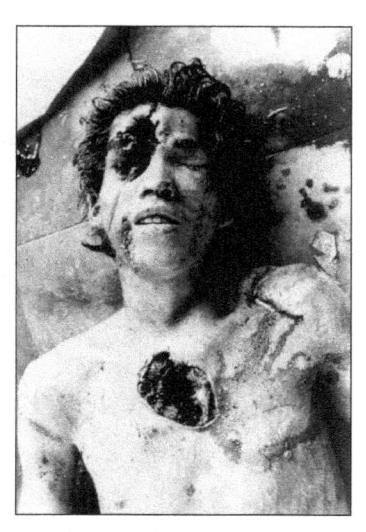

Picture of a tortured and murdered man in El Salvador[121]

Hearing the tortured men speak, I was shocked. Seeing the signs of their torture on their bodies and realizing the pain they must have endured, I broke into tears. "My Lord," I said to myself. "I came to comfort, and now I need it myself. I, the would-be ecclesiastical diplomat, reduced to tears!"[122]

The archbishop put an arm on my shoulder. He told me nothing could mean more to him than my tears, which made me one with his suffering people. Immediately, he spoke words of forgiveness. I will never forget that. This is what I recall him saying:

> Doctor, we have to be understanding. Our persecutors have never seen the church taking up the cause of the poor as its highest priority. This frightens them. Until now no one had truly challenged their privilege. Now, we, the church, appear to them as their most formidable enemy. That's why we must pray for them, that God may forgive them and convert them.[123]

Jorge and Monseñor Romero

After that, there was no hesitation on my part. I pledged to him my unconditional support and the certain solidarity of the church councils that had sent me.

Over the next few years, I would make several trips to El Salvador. On one particular trip in early 1979, the monseñor invited me to accompany him in celebrating the Week of Prayer for Christian Unity. What was to be a series of festive Catholic-Protestant worship services turned instead into a succession of funeral liturgies.

Scarcely two hours after my arrival on January 20, I was ushered into the Emmanuel Baptist Church, crowded with ecumenical Christians. I reached the chancel, just as the host pastor, Miguel Tomás Castro García, was expressing his condolences to the Catholics present. The news had reached him by phone a few minutes earlier that the National Guard, using a tank, a jeep, and a machine gun in the early hours of that day, had suddenly broken into a Catholic retreat center and killed Octavio Ortiz Luna, the priest leading the retreat, and four youngsters in attendance. The congregation was stunned. Some groaned in anger; others broke out in sobs.

**Jorge speaking at Emmanuel Baptist Church,
San Salvador, Saturday, January 20, 1979**

The next day, Sunday, I stood next to Monseñor Romero on the steps of the Metropolitan Catholic Cathedral. Immediately below us were the five open coffins. Surrounding us were all the priests and nuns of the archdiocese. Beyond the coffins were some twenty-five thousand Catholics and Protestants crowded into the national plaza. I offered my condolences:

> I am able to listen to the priest, Octavio Ortiz Luna, speak from eternity, from the place where there is no more weeping or mourning or death. He speaks to each one of us, his sisters and brothers who continue to journey here on earth: Now I rejoice in what I have suffered for you and in my flesh I complete what was lacking in the afflictions of Christ, afflictions that were offered up for the good of his body: the Church.[124]

ÓSCAR ROMERO ¡PRESENTE!

The crowd on January 21, 1979, the day of the funeral of Father Luna and the other martyrs

Standing before that multitude, I realized what was needed. I pled with them to forgive us, the Christians in the United States, for the measure in which we had allowed our nation to support a system that manufactures poor people and rewards oppressors in the name of national security. The ovation that followed was deafening, and also sobering. It symbolized a plea: that our nation desist from placing its confidence in dealers of death.[125]

As the archbishop spoke that morning, I felt myself caught up in his faith, the faith of his flock, and the faith of the other martyrs of the Christian community. Romero said:

> We pray for the conversion of our persecutors. With our love we pray, Father forgive them for they know not what they do. Not to pray that way is to give way to revenge and further violence. But ours is not the cheap forgiveness. We hereby excommunicate the intellectual

and material authors of yesterday's killings and the previous killings of three other priests and of the multitude of the faithful who said no to injustice. But even as we excommunicate them, we pray for their conversion. This is why as we see these five bodies of martyrs before us, we think more of resurrection than assassination.[126]

I needed desperately to hear these words of wisdom. Otherwise, I would have granted the enemy that double victory of which the archbishop spoke. Now, instead of cursing my enemy, I would pray for him. I would see myself in him and ask God to forgive us both. Surely, if Monseñor Romero could forgive the perpetrators of such violent crimes, I could forgive not only others, but myself for my many inadequacies.[127]

Once I got to know the monseñor better, he invited me for a weeklong journey into the countryside where we would visit small Bible study groups called base ecclesial communities. At one of the stops, the community members gathered on the grass. That community was reading about the Exodus, and I asked Archbishop Romero if I could interrupt to ask a question. He joked, "Absolutely. You are traveling with the boss." And then he said to the group, "He wants to ask you a question. Will you let him?"

They said, "Oh, yeah, yeah."

I said, "I notice you are studying the story of Exodus. Let me ask you, if this story were being rewritten today, who would be the Pharaoh?"

They answered, "General Romero!" [the president].

"And, if he is the Pharaoh, who would Moses be?"

A heavy-set lady looked at me and said, "At the risk of embarrassing your travel companion, his name is Óscar Romero."

I asked, "And what would be the crossing of the Red Sea?"

Another person said, "The Revolution." I noticed the bishop stiffened a bit when he heard that.

The final question was, "What would be the promised land?"

A very decisive-looking man said, "The land we will never have, but we are on our way to possessing."[128]

During my sojourns in El Salvador, as a Protestant I felt grateful to have been so completely accepted by Catholics. Those days, when I was working so hard to build unity among divided religious groups in the United States, it was sometimes hard to return to New York, where we continued to struggle with doctrinal divisions. These petty conflicts at home often seemed ridiculous when contrasted to the tragedies happening in El Salvador.

Jorge and Monseñor Romero visiting the town of Arcatao in 1979[129]

By January 1980, threats on Romero's life were a daily occurrence. On the final evening of my last week with him, he and I were being driven back to San Salvador. In the privacy of the back seat of the car, I asked if he was going to take any measure to protect himself. His reply was heart-rending. He said he had no appetite for martyrdom and had never been more in love with life. His flock had never been more spiritually alive. Of course, he would be grateful to God for even a few more years. But he would not hide. When his own people risked everything by following him, his own personal security was out of the question. I can still hear his concluding remark, "It all comes down to laying down life for one's friends. That is the kind of love I owe my people." It was a reverential moment, best honored by silence and tears.[130]

In February 1980, he was invited to Belgium to receive an honorary doctorate from the Catholic University of Louvain. When he received the degree, he took the opportunity to denounce the persecution of his church members who had worked to help the poor:

> In less than three years over fifty priests have been attacked, threatened, calumniated. Six are already martyrs—they were murdered. Some have been tortured and others expelled (from the country). Nuns have also been persecuted. The archdiocesan radio station and educational institutions that are Catholic, or of a Christian inspiration, have been attacked, threatened, intimidated, even bombed.... There have been threats, arrests, tortures, murders, numbering in the hundreds and thousands.[131]

Archbishop Romero receiving an honoris causa doctorate from the University of Louvian, Belgium, February 2, 1980[132]

That same month, on February 17, he wrote to President Jimmy Carter pleading with him to give no more arms to the government of El Salvador. Here are excerpts from the letter:

Dear Mr. President,

... I am very concerned by the news that the government of the United States is planning to further El Salvador's arms race by sending military equipment and advisers to "train three Salvadoran battalions in logistics, communications and intelligence." If this information from the newspapers is correct, instead of favoring greater justice and peace in El Salvador, your government's contribution will undoubtedly sharpen the injustice and the repression inflicted on the organized people, whose struggle has often been for respect for their most basic human rights.

… given that as a Salvadoran and archbishop of the archdiocese of San Salvador, I have an obligation to see that faith and justice reign in my country, I ask you, if you truly want to defend human rights:

- To forbid that military aid be given to the Salvadoran government;
- To guarantee that your government will not intervene directly or indirectly, with military, economic, diplomatic or other pressures, in determining the destiny of the Salvadoran people.[133]

Archbishop Romero's main point was: "Please do not send weapons. They will be used for more repression against my people."[134]

National Guard arresting protesters in San Salvador[135]

**Women murdered by a death squad
in Apopa, El Salvador**[136]

On Sunday, March 23, 1980, five weeks after sending his letter to President Carter, Romero spoke directly to the soldiers in his radio homily from the cathedral.

> Do not obey your superiors when they order you to kill. You are killing your brothers and sisters. In the name of God, in the name of these suffering people whose laments rise to heaven, each day more tumultuous, I beg of you, I ask of you, I order you, in the name of God, stop the repression![137]

Romero's followers were jubilant. The generals were furious. They called him a communist and a traitor to his people.

Archbishop Romero showing his passion[138]

The next afternoon, Monday, March 24, the archbishop officiated at a memorial Mass for Doña Sarita Pinto. She was the mother of his friend Jorge Pinto, who owned a weekly newspaper called *El Independiente*. The headquarters of his newspaper had recently been bombed.[139] Putting aside the death threats of the day, Romero permitted the Mass to be announced in the newspapers.

The Mass was held in the small chapel of the Divina Providencia Hospital, a center run by Mexican Carmelite nuns, and the place where the archbishop lived. Typical of El Salvador, it was a very hot day; therefore, the wing-shaped chapel doors were open.

Like Jesus, Doña Sarita had given of herself generously, blessing everyone she touched. In his homily, Archbishop Romero urged everyone to follow her example. As he pointed to the bread and the cup, he ended with a reflection:

> We receive here the body of the Lord who offered himself for the redemption of the world. May His body and blood given for us nourish us in such a way that we, too, may give our body and blood like Christ, to bring justice and peace to our people. That is what Doña Sarita did. Let us, then, join ourselves to her in prayer, in the same hope and faith by which she lived.[140]

At that very moment, a thin, red-bearded man in the passenger seat of a red Volkswagen Passat raised an assault rifle and fired a single .22-caliber bullet into Archbishop Romero's heart.[141] He had been standing behind the altar of the chapel. He fell at the foot of the large crucifix behind him. The stunned congregants remained crouching in the pews. In spite of obvious danger, several nuns ran to him. He was lying face down, so they turned him over onto his back. Blood gushed from his mouth and nose, as he mumbled words of forgiveness. The bullet had entered the left side of his chest. Blood saturated his robes. Friends whisked him outside to a panel truck and took him to the nearest emergency room. At the hospital, one of the nuns, a nurse, tried to start a transfusion. When she realized his veins had collapsed, she cried out, "Oh no, his body is broken. His blood is drained. There is none left!"[142]

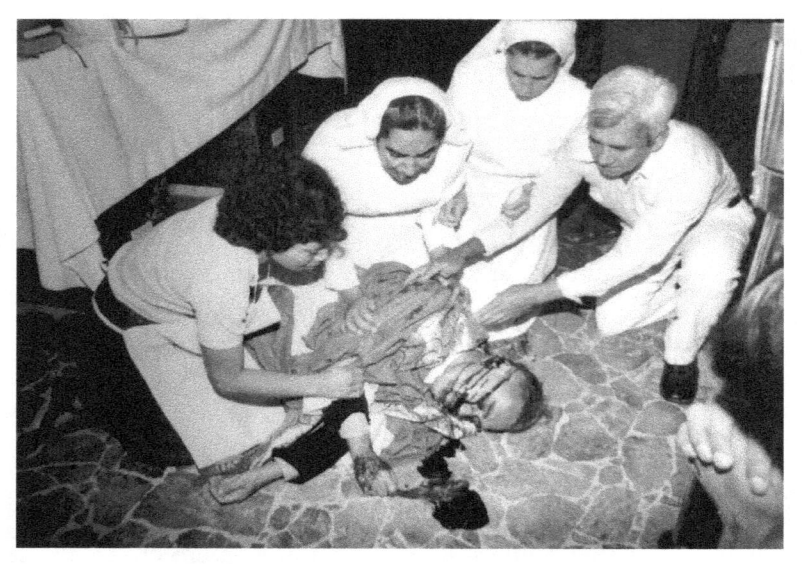

Moments after Monseñor Romero was assassinated[143]

Óscar Romero died while being held by this nun. The preacher of beatitudes, fearless prophet, and kindest pastor was no more. Through their tears, his friends began to question, "How could he die now when we needed him the most?" And, "If he was not spared, is there hope for any of us who believed in him and his cause?"[144]

ÓSCAR ROMERO ¡PRESENTE!

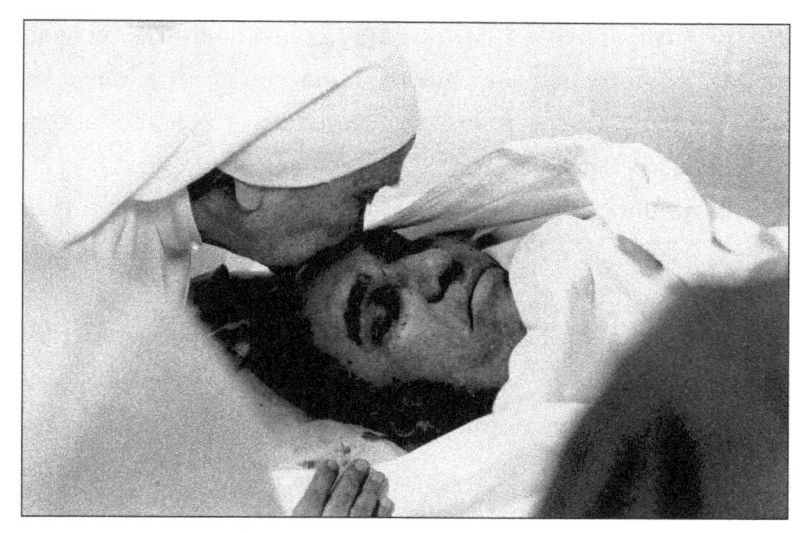

Nun kissing the head of Archbishop Romero, March 24, 1980, at the Hospital of Divine Providence, San Salvador[145]

One hour later, my dear friend Miguel Tomás, pastor of Emmanuel Baptist Church, called me from San Salvador. In a voice heavy with tears, he blurted out the awful news, "Jorge, our archbishop has been killed." I wept my heart out.[146]

When pastor Miguel phoned me, I was in Washington, D.C., to testify the following day before a House Appropriations subcommittee. It was faced with the challenge of whether to renew U.S. military assistance to El Salvador. It was an exercise in futility to try to stop the subcommittee's determination to resume military intervention. I was preparing to present testimony on behalf of the National Council of Churches on the issue.

After I testified, six out of nine representatives voted in favor of not renewing aid. We had won, we thought. However, officers were there from the CIA and the Defense Intelligence Agency. They asked for a behind-the-scenes conference, and the vote was reversed. I wept openly. I expressed my determination never again to remain silent when the issue of military appropriations came up, particularly appropriations that were made to regimes notorious for their violations of human rights.[147]

Once resumed, U.S. military involvement in El Salvador grew to the third-largest military aid program in the world at that time. From 1982 to 1989, the Salvadoran government was given an average of a million dollars a day. The death toll eventually reached in the civil war was more than 75,000 Salvadorans, mostly civilians murdered by the military—in the name of fighting "communists" like Óscar Romero.[148]

Soldiers in Llopango, El Salvador, being instructed by a U.S. Special Forces adviser on how to use an M-203 grenade launcher[149]

Soon after I testified, Bill Wipfler, director of the Human Rights Office at the National Council of Churches, called to ask me to put together a U.S. delegation to travel to San Salvador for the archbishop's funeral.[150] On Palm Sunday weekend, approximately fifty church dignitaries from twenty countries, including Latin America, Europe, and the United States, flew to San Salvador to honor our friend and mentor.

On the radiantly brilliant day of Archbishop Romero's funeral Mass, an altar was improvised at the top of the stairs leading to the main entrance of the old, unfinished cathedral adjacent to the National Palace, headquarters of the Salvadoran government. Archbishop Romero's coffin, which was protected by a six-foot metal fence, had been placed at the foot of the stairs. I stood at the top of the stairs near the pope's representative, Cardinal Ernesto Corripio Ahumada, archbishop of Mexico City. The plaza was jammed with the archbishop's flock—well over 200,000 people—mostly poor people on whose behalf his voice had been so compelling.

Nuns paying their respects to Monseñor Romero in the days before his funeral

The crowd outside the cathedral was estimated at a quarter of a million people on the day of Monseñor Romero's funeral, March 30, 1980. Photograph is looking toward the National Palace from the cathedral.[151]

ÓSCAR ROMERO ¡PRESENTE!

Due to the size of the crowd, Romero's coffin had to be moved to the steps of the Metropolitan Cathedral. Notice the huge banner of Romero on the front of the church.[152]

As the Mass continued, Cardinal Corripio paid tribute to the martyred archbishop. Just as he was paraphrasing an often-heard teaching of Monseñor Romero—"neither truth nor justice can be killed by violence"—he was stunned speechless, as we all were, by the thunderous detonation of a bomb.

Jorge is the bearded man behind Cardinal Corripio's right shoulder on the steps of the Metropolitan Cathedral of San Salvador moments before the first explosion[153]

The explosion occurred at the far corner of the National Palace. I stared open-mouthed at the palace and saw leaping fire and thick, pluming smoke as if the pavement were aflame. The crowd stampeded away from the palace. There was the immediate sound of gunfire. Like a massive wave, thousands headed for the only possible shelter, the empty cathedral behind us.[154]

**Bomb exploding from the area near the
National Palace in the plaza outside
the Metropolitan Cathedral**[155]

We were packed so tightly into the space that smaller people—mostly women, jammed between the bodies of larger men—began suffocating. I felt someone tugging on my robe sleeve and turned to see a woman gasping for breath. Because I was wearing a gown and a hood, she thought I was a priest. Knowing she wanted last rites, I made the sign of the cross and whispered words of forgiveness. She died instantly. Others helped me lift her body up over our heads to a place outside the cathedral. There, she was put on a pile, with the others who had also suffocated to death. All my life, I have been a pathetic claustrophobic. Being trapped in a small space had always been my own private nightmare. That day, I kept panic away by looking after my neighbors, praying with them and speaking calm words of comfort—some learned from Monseñor.[156]

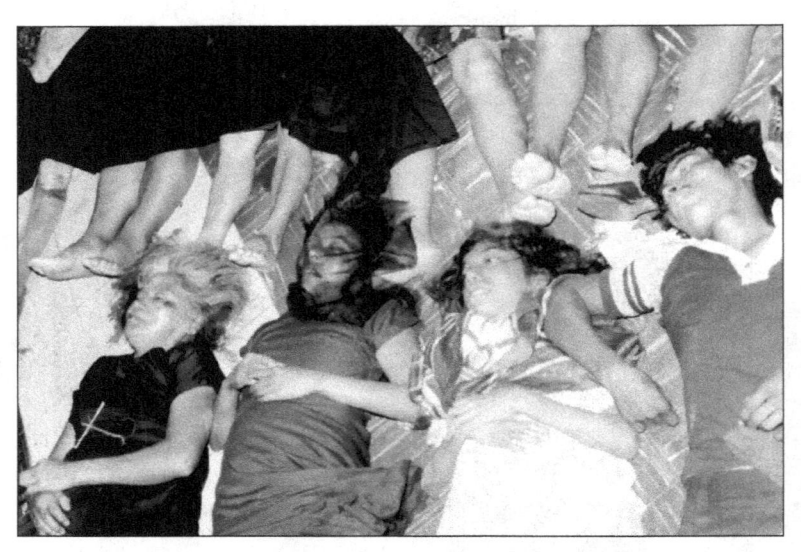

Bodies of people, most of whom died of suffocation during the funeral service

Suddenly, astonishingly, over the bombs, guns, and prayers, we heard the sound of cheering. Something was being carried forward by multiple hands over our heads. It took a while for this object to come into my view, but a chant that was joined by everyone in the cathedral announced its arrival: "*¡El Pueblo unido jamas* *sera vencido! ¡El pueblo unido jamas sera vencido!*" (The people united will never be defeated!) What the chant was announcing, I eventually could see, was the coffin of the archbishop, held aloft by fingertips, making its perilous way into this sanctuary of faith and terror, to its final resting place. Despite the violence outside, a group from the cathedral had gone out and down the steps to retrieve the coffin. Even in death, the archbishop had transformed despair into courage.[157]

Inside the cathedral after the violence

Jorge after Archbishop Romero's funeral service

When the shooting died down, Samuel Ruiz, the bishop of Chiapas, and I walked out of the cathedral arm in arm. We were shattered when we saw a small boy hugging the dead body of his mother in the pile of the women who had suffocated. I wept, and Bishop Ruiz, who was watching, called out, "Those murderers have crucified Him again, but He will rise again!"

ÓSCAR ROMERO ¡PRESENTE!

Jorge and Bishop Samuel Ruiz of Chiapas after the madness

That night, we church representatives from around the world met to piece together what had happened. The government was already denying involvement, so we decided to put our eyewitness account in writing. And all twenty-three of us signed the document.[158]

The next day, we discovered dramatically different accounts in Salvadoran and U.S. newspapers. They stated that the explosions and gunfire were from radical leftists, and that the military and government were in no way involved.

Óscar Romero lived life to the fullest by practicing the Beatitudes, which Jesus proclaimed in the Sermon on the Mount. Because of this, thousands claimed that death could not hold him. Instead of mourning Monseñor, people in the barrios and churches cheered him. They shouted: "¡Óscar Romero, *presente!*" "¡Óscar Romero, *presente!*" Since then, many more people have joined him and paid homage to his good adventure by seeking justice for those who have been wronged, reaching out to the impoverished, and helping those who cannot help themselves.[159]

My friendship with Óscar Romero has remained forever central to me. More than anyone I have ever known, Monseñor brought Jesus alive. As I said in my address in San Salvador, on the steps of the Metropolitan Cathedral on the twentieth anniversary of his death: "Together with thousands of Salvadorans, I have seen Jesus. His name is Óscar Arnulfo Romero."[160]

Jorge praying at Monseñor's crypt on the twentieth anniversary of his death

CHAPTER TWELVE

Deeply Engaged

*The destruction caused by good people who
are indifferent and uninformed
can more than equal the evil of people with bad intentions.*

—Jorge Lara-Braud,
in *Awakening Courage*

In 1980, I moved from New York to Atlanta, where I took a new post as the director of the Council on Theology and Culture of the Presbyterian Church in the United States (PCUS), popularly known as the Southern Presbyterian Church. At first, I was reluctant to move from an ecumenical position, which involved worldwide service, to a denominational one. While my positions at the National Council of Churches and as an officer on the World Council empowered me to speak out for people in Central America, and beyond, I feared this new position would narrow my scope.

However, soon after I arrived in Atlanta, I became deeply engaged in coordinating a study document for the Presbyterian Church on a subject I truly cared about: the unique relationship between Christians and Jews. We hoped that our paper would be adopted by the General Assembly, a gathering of the entire Presbyterian Church, which would take place in Atlanta in 1983. If adopted, it could serve as an official study paper, not only for Presbyterians, but for other denominations as well. We wanted to show that the Romans, not the Jews, were primarily responsible for crucifying Jesus. Unfortunately, many people were convinced that the Jews had crucified him. This unfounded conclusion was one of the primary causes for prejudice against the Jewish people.

Prior to 1983, the Presbyterian Church was divided into two parts, the Northern and Southern branches. Although members representing the Southern branch were committed to the study document, members from the Northern branch were uniformly opposed. When it became apparent that a majority of the General

Assembly Committee would recommend the paper's rejection, I proposed instead that it be given to a reconstituted panel made up of the original drafters plus individuals who had opposed it. This is what ultimately happened. The new official study document was finally published in 1987 by the reunited church, the Presbyterian Church (USA). It was entitled "A Theological Understanding of the Relationship between Christians and Jews."[161]

During 1981, while I was working on the document, my sister Cachuy called from Mexico City to tell me our brother was dying. Luis had become a nationally recognized banker and a prominent export-import dealer. He was not only genial and debonair but quintessentially macho. He had married twice and had five children. When his export-import business collapsed overnight, his whole life went downhill and he became an alcoholic. Later many in the family would blame alcoholism for his death. However, I thought he had died from that kind of cynicism expressed by the author of Ecclesiastes: "There is no new thing under the sun." For Luis at the end, there was no horizon of hope, just the gathering gloom of a descent into hell. He died on April 24. I pray I may have helped him, as I did my best to comfort him, even through the brutalizing fumes of alcohol. At times after his death, I was brought up short by a lightninglike realization—he was no longer. And yet he was. I prayed for his resurrection and could see him risen beyond fumes to the radiance of God.[162]

In September 1982, while I was working on the report about Christians and Jews, I received a letter from Gretchen Shartle, a woman in Austin, Texas, who knew my friend Frank Sugeno. I had met Frank, a Japanese American priest, in the late 1960s when he participated in a January Seminar organized by the Hispanic-American Institute. Frank wanted us to meet because he knew we were both committed to ending U.S.-sponsored repression in Central America. Since I made frequent trips to Austin, he asked Gretchen to write me, suggesting we three get together. I was so busy when I received her letter that I told Phyllis, my secretary in Atlanta, that I had no time to meet new people and asked her to toss the letter.

Fortunately, she disobeyed me. As I was leaving for Austin in April 1983, to present the Heinsohn Lectures on Central America at the University Methodist Church, Phyllis put Gretchen's letter in my briefcase and reminded me to call her. Soon after arriving, I invited Gretchen to meet me downtown. She had just returned from her first trip to Nicaragua and was passionate about the Sandinistas' struggle.

The next day, preceding the lectures, my sermon was on "Lilies of the Field." In-between services, I invited Gretchen and her fifteen-year-old daughter, Greta, to accompany me to the pastor's office, where I described Archbishop Romero's funeral three years before. They were horrified to hear about the violence in the plaza during the funeral, and about the many women who had suffocated as they crowded into the cathedral for safety.

Greta and Gretchen in the mid-1980s

Between April 17 and 19, I gave a total of thirteen lectures and interviews on El Salvador and Nicaragua, a schedule that resulted in a severe migraine. I took part of a day to rest and be with Gretchen before returning to Atlanta. That's when she hesitantly told me how much she had loved my sermon based on the "Lilies of the Field": "Oh, that was a wonderful sermon. I feel so proud of you as though you were my best friend!"[163] Her transparent way of expressing herself warmed my heart. I was moved not only by Gretchen but also by her daughter. I had always wished for a daughter, and as time went on, Greta began to seem like my own child.

Since we first met, Gretchen had been telling me about the Fourth of July trip to Nicaragua planned by the Carolina Interfaith Task Force. She encouraged me to come and to invite other church leaders. I had visited Nicaragua several times as a Presbyterian representative, so I was well acquainted with that country's political struggles.

It was shocking to see the parallels between Nicaragua of the twentieth century and the United States of the eighteenth century. Just as Britain was the oppressor of the United States, America was now the oppressor of Nicaragua. Both countries had played David-like roles against their respective Goliaths.

United under the rebel leadership of Augusto César Sandino, Nicaraguans fought passionately in the late 1920s and early 1930s against American interventions. In 1932, the United States created a National Guard in Nicaragua, a combined military and police force, to safeguard American interests. Anastasio Somoza García was appointed to be its director.

Sandino and his men relaxed somewhat when the U.S. Marines finally left Nicaragua in 1933. They retreated to the northern mountains. Unfortunately, Sandino was tricked the following year. Having been assured of his safety by Anthony Bliss Lane, the U.S. ambassador to Nicaragua, Sandino came down from the mountains to work out a peace agreement with General Somoza. On February 21, 1934, Somoza ordered the officers of the National Guard to kill Sandino. They yanked him and two of his generals from his car, took them to a nearby field, and shot them dead. Afterward, Somoza claimed he had received approval from Lane. The National Guard then massacred Sandino's troops and many of their families who were establishing cooperatives in a northern rural area.[164]

Nicaraguan revolutionary Augusto César Sandino[165]

In 1936, General Somoza manipulated his way into the presidency of Nicaragua, so that he then would have total control. As director of the National Guard, Anastasio Somoza, with the full backing of the United States, continued to be in charge of the police and the military. His family established a dictatorship and a family dynasty that would rule Nicaragua for more than forty years. President Franklin Roosevelt is alleged to have said in 1939, "Somoza may be a son of a bitch, but he's our son of a bitch."[166]

After the 1972 Managua earthquake in which 10,000 people died and 300,000 were left homeless, the United States and other countries sent millions of dollars to help rebuild Managua.[167] At that time, General Somoza's son, Anastasio Somoza Debayle (nicknamed "Tachito"), became the de facto ruler of Nicaragua. Soon after he misappropriated these funds for himself. Knowledge of Tachito's embezzlement finally began to awaken people in both Nicaragua and the United States to the corruption of the Somoza regime.[168]

A shift in the Catholic Church filled the Nicaraguan people with hope, just as it did their Salvadoran counterparts. After Vatican II, the Roman Catholic Church began to follow Scripture more closely by helping the poor. Throughout Central and South America, people started to participate in grass-roots Christian groups—base ecclesial communities—similar to the one I visited in El Salvador with Monseñor Romero. Reading Bible stories and facing their struggles together in community groups empowered Nicaraguans. Like the Israelites in the story of the Red Sea that opened for Moses and allowed them to cross over and gain their freedom, the Sandinistas became hopeful that they too could stand up and free themselves from Somoza's tyrannical rule.

Although their leader, Sandino, had been assassinated decades before, his fiery spirit still burned in people's hearts.

Until the late 1970s, few Americans realized that the United States government had been supporting an unscrupulous dictatorship in Nicaragua. The first U.S. president to recognize the corruption of the Somoza regime, then act on this reality, was Jimmy Carter. After warning the Somoza dynasty in 1977, he terminated aid to Nicaragua in 1978 because of its human rights violations. When Somoza lost U.S. support, the regime's power declined. The majority of the Nicaraguan people were overjoyed.

Step by step, more Americans and Nicaraguans learned the truth about the Somoza regime. One powerful event caught many people's attention. On June 20, 1979, Americans watched the ruthless killing of Bill Stewart, an ABC TV correspondent in Managua.[169] Stewart was pulled out of his car, forced to kneel, then shot through the head by members of the National Guard who had seen him filming compromising scenes. What the guardsmen did not realize was that Stewart's camera crew filmed the killing, which was then aired on television to a global audience. This display of utter contempt for human life could not be erased from the hearts and minds of millions of Americans. It also helped to motivate Nicaraguans in their fight against the Somoza regime.[170]

Finally, Nicaraguans, heartened by the withdrawal of U.S. support and encouraged by the Catholic Church, overthrew the Somozas. The official date of their triumph was July 19, 1979. Their victory was costly. Out of a population of 3.5 million people, approximately 50,000 people were killed and 300,000 Nicaraguans were wounded.[171] One-fifth of the population was left homeless.[172]

Walter Cronkite commenting on the death of Bill Stewart on the CBS Evening News[173]

To me, the most significant part of the Sandinistas' role in their forty-five-year struggle against the Somoza dynasty was the way they handled the years immediately following their victory. The new government took on the Somozas' $1.6 billion debt to the United States.[174] They also focused on forgiveness and discouraged vengeance. They executed no one, handed out relatively short sentences to military personnel for past war crimes, and permitted no acts of revenge, even against officers of the National Guard.[175] Tomás Borge, who became the minister of the interior in 1979, exemplified this spirit of forgiveness. Right away, he overhauled the prison system and made it much more humane.[176] The Sandinistas also devoted significant resources to health care, infrastructure, housing for the poor, the arts, and literacy. According to Thomas W. Walker and Christine J. Wade, "The 1980 Literacy Crusade lowered the national illiteracy rate from fifty-one percent to thirteen percent."[177] Dr. Ulrike Hanemann reported that "the new government sent over 95,000 Nicaraguans from cities to remote areas to teach people to read and write. Even some children as young as twelve left their homes to live with other families in rural areas to teach the adults and children."[178]

I could not imagine children that young having the courage to leave their families, in order to live with and teach strangers in remote areas. Nor could I imagine their parents being willing to send them.

Even as Nicaraguans were still celebrating their new day, most of the former National Guard fled across Nicaragua's northern border into Honduras. Soon after, in 1981, following Ronald Reagan's election as U.S. president, his administration employed the CIA to recruit, pay, arm, equip, and organize the former National Guard as counterrevolutionaries—hence the name "Contras." Their average pay was roughly ten times what local Hondurans earned. By February of 1981, the U.S. government was funding more than six thousand Contras living in Honduran refugee camps.[179]

While the new Sandinista government was intent on rebuilding the country, the Contras were destroying their work. Many people in the United States were deceived about what was really happening through news stories designed to frighten them about the encroachment of communism via Cuba into Nicaragua.

I arrived in Managua with our Atlanta group on July 1, 1983. We brought a large banner declaring: "*¡Tu libertad es nuestra libertad!*" (Your freedom is our freedom). Soon after arriving, I was asked to be the leader of our group consisting of 150 people from all over the United States. This was probably because I was bilingual, had a good grasp of the political and cultural background, and knew many of the Sandinista representatives.

Banner made by the Atlanta members on the trip

The purpose of our trip was to stand in solidarity with the Sandinistas and to inform Americans about Nicaragua's struggle. The Sandinistas had planned for us to go to Jalapa, on the border between Honduras and Nicaragua, a place where numerous Sandinistas had been killed by Contras. This was risky. Some in our group were cautious, including Gretchen. Her daughter Greta was afraid and asked her to be very wary on the trip. Therefore, my first task was to work with the Sandinista leaders to ensure everyone's safety.

Two days before we went to Jalapa, I addressed a binational group in a Managua Baptist church. Afterward, I was amazed to see my dear friend, Henri Nouwen, the Dutch priest and well-known author. Since Henri wanted to join us on our trip to Jalapa, we had to get an additional security clearance for him.

Consequently, I spent hours working on security details with the Sandinista leaders for our upcoming trip. The safety of each and every person in our group was of paramount importance to them as well as to us.

Before leaving, all 150 of us attended Mass in the Church of Santa María de Los Angeles on the Fourth of July. Guitarists played and we danced with the families. We rejoiced with them not only for their triumph over the Somoza regime, but also for establishing programs to benefit the people.

Henri Nouwen (left, with head bowed) and Jorge (right, wearing cross) at the Church of Santa María de Los Angeles in Managua

Toward the end of the service, Tomás Borge arrived. He touched our hearts when he said: "Me loves you." I had met with Borge several times before this trip and was moved by his courage. He and his wife had been imprisoned during the revolution. Even though his wife had been tortured to death, Borge refused to return violence for violence. After the revolution, he calmed

Nicaraguans who were determined to lynch members of Somoza's National Guard. He said that if we were to treat them the way they treated us, the revolution would have been for nothing.[180] He wrote: "My personal revenge will be to say to you 'good morning' without beggars in the streets, when instead of jailing you I intend to shake the sorrow from your eyes."[181]

Tomás Borge

At the end of the church celebration, Capitán Sanchez, who worked closely with Borge, met with us. He assured us we would be safe on the trip to Jalapa the next day. Like Borge, Sanchez said, "I don't know much English but I love you." He then added, "Better for several of us to die than one of you!" After hearing the captain's assurance that we would be safe and that Henri Nouwen would be joining us, Gretchen decided she would go.

On July 5 at six in the morning, we piled into four rickety buses and started our ten-hour trip to Jalapa. What struck me as we passed through little towns on our way were the women and children framed in doorways—so lovely—themselves like prayers for peace.

Loading buses for the trip to Jalapa

When the buses stopped in Estelí just long enough for people to drink a beer or a soda, Gretchen surprised me. She had mixed feelings about my role in the spotlight. To take me down a peg or two, she laughed, then sang: "Jesus Christ, Superstar, who in the world do you think you are?"

Greeted by thunder and rain, we arrived in Jalapa at four in the afternoon. Right away, we noticed the Contras' fortifications atop the hills to the north of us. We could also see Contra soldiers standing just above the school buildings where we would be staying. We had dinner on the local school's basketball court, then headed to the town meeting hall, which was built like an amphitheater. I found myself in the center leading our group in cheers as the local people joined in calling out together: *"No pasarán"*

(They will not get through—referring to the Contras), and "*¡El pueblo unido jamás será vencido!*" (The people united will never be defeated).

Contra soldiers on the hill above the high school where we stayed

Amidst the confusion of arriving in Jalapa, I missed an announcement to beware of the water barrels sitting just outside the town. They had been dosed with Paraquat for killing mosquitos. I took some of the liquid into my hands and washed my face with it. My face immediately turned purple.

Before retiring that night, Gretchen and I decided to explore. My bright red face was still stinging from the Paraquat. Dressed in dirty clothes, we tromped through the mud and joked with the Sandinista soldiers who passed us in jeeps, "We wondered if you might think we were Contras?" They laughed and responded, "No way, you don't look like Contras at all."[182]

The rain had stopped. We sat on two rocks and talked. Blessed by the stars and the Milky Way, it seemed an improbable place for war. We both lamented the painful struggle of the Nicaraguan people. They faced huge odds—a tiny group of committed people trying to stand up against the Contras who were backed by the most powerful country in the world, the United States of America.

It was tough to realize that our country was supporting counterrevolutionaries who were bent on destroying the schools, health centers, and the entire infrastructure that had been painstakingly built by the Sandinistas. It horrified me to hear details regarding the cruelty of the Contras. That night Gretchen told me what she had learned from Pedrarius, a young doctor whom she met during her first trip to Nicaragua. She visited with him soon after he had returned from the battle front where he and fifteen other professors had volunteered to care for the wounded. He told her that the Contras were known to hideously brutalize the men they captured. They often cut off their testicles, then slit their abdomens with bayonets. Pedrarius said that when the Contras passed through villages, they killed children, old people, and any who were in their path. And here we were, that night, almost within earshot of those same people.

We slept on the cold floors of two public high school buildings: one designated for men, the other for women. It was so uncomfortable I never fell asleep. At dawn when I heard the sound of horses' hooves followed by mariachis, I hurriedly got up. I discovered they had come to announce a morning Mass to be held on the basketball court. The electrifying music had moved Gretchen to dance off to the side after the Mass. I laughed when I saw Henri Nouwen pulling her into the center as he said, "Give your dancing to God!"[183]

The school buildings where we slept

Afterward, the mothers and wives of Sandinista soldiers took us to a nearby field where their sons, brothers, and husbands had recently been killed. I remember how distraught they were, not only because they had lost their loved ones, but also because the Contras had cut the bodies into pieces; therefore, they could not be buried whole. Some of the local people believed a person's dismembered body could not be received into heaven. While in the field, we were further dismayed to find U.S. bullet cartridges on the ground left by the Contras during one of their earlier attacks. We linked hands with the women and made a human chain to symbolize a protective barrier between Jalapa and the Honduran border. We wanted to commiserate with them and lend them our support for a few hours. Then, one by one, members of our group asked the mothers to forgive us for allowing the U.S. government to do so much harm. Their family members' deaths, in that very spot, were orchestrated by our own government. We were humbled and grateful that each one of them forgave each one of us.

Mothers from whom we asked forgiveness

Their forgiveness moved us to promise ourselves that we would try with all our hearts to stop this hideous violence. We felt partly responsible because our government officials had been elected by us, the people. The president of our country, Ronald Reagan, had needlessly engineered the killings of so many during his misguided crusade against communism. Like the Sandinistas, we felt overwhelmed.

Even the U.S. news media had been strongly influenced by our government. Top *New York Times* journalists, like Ray Bonner, lost their jobs because they refused to write dishonest reports that corroborated the views of the Reagan administration. Bonner said he was dismissed because he was criticized by the *Wall Street Journal* and State Department officials. He was fired for being "soft on communism."[184] No wonder the American people were not well informed about U.S. support of the Contras and about the Sandinistas' struggle to help the Nicaraguan people. American news sources were cowing to the pressure of the administration, which was funneling propaganda.

Our July 1983 trip inspired many of us to spread the word and try to turn our country around. The odds, however, were against us. How could we, a few ordinary people armed with only our ideals and firsthand experience, bring about a significant change when leaders of the United States, including our president, were opposed? In the face of such power, our temptation was to give up before we even started, but how could we turn our backs on our friends who were being killed every day?

Many of us envisioned a continuous international presence in Nicaragua composed of American and international volunteers. This soon led to the founding of Witness for Peace (WFP). These volunteers would put their lives at risk while spending periods of time on the border between Honduras and Nicaragua. By being there, they could make firsthand reports about the Contras' violence, thereby offering a reliable news source for people in the United States and beyond.

The Contras would not want to be implicated in killing U.S. citizens; nor would they want Americans to witness their aggressive forays into Nicaragua. We spoke to Tomás Borge and others about the idea. At first they were opposed, because they did not want any of us to be killed. Finally, we persuaded Borge, and other Sandinista leaders, to relent. Faith-based peace activists then began the necessary steps to set up Witness for Peace.

While I never served as a volunteer, I strongly endorsed the program's nonviolence. Step by step, Witness for Peace established an ongoing international presence in Nicaragua and Honduras. After a few years, volunteers signed up for one-year commitments. Eventually, WFP spread to hotspots in other countries. It eventually sent thousands of volunteers to Latin America and the Caribbean.

Of course, not everyone was able to go to Nicaragua for several months to volunteer with Witness for Peace. Therefore, Gretchen and I considered other ways to engage church leaders and inspire their congregations to become involved firsthand. Frank Sugeno recommended we contact national leaders in the Episcopal Church. We also invited prominent Catholic, Presbyterian, and Lutheran representatives throughout the United States to join us on nonpartisan, fact-finding trips to Central America. There they could see the realities with their own eyes.

From 1984 to 1987, through the support of a charitable foundation and the Central American Refugee Center (CARECEN),[185] we sent more than thirty-five prominent church leaders to visit El Salvador, Honduras, and Nicaragua.[186] Participants were responsible for their lodging and travel. Before their departure, they took part in orientation sessions in the United States where I presented an overview of the political and religious dimensions of the conflict. Once in Central America, I led the meetings with the political groups, members of the press, local church leaders, and American ambassadors.

Jorge speaking at an orientation

Polls in the United States indicated as early as 1984 that public opinion had begun to turn against the Contras. We were heartened when, in 1985, the U.S. Congress passed the Boland Amendment, which forbade help to the Contras by all U.S. government agencies. The Reagan administration nevertheless managed to continue to send the Contras money through illegal covert operations.

John Pyle, the canon pastor at the National Cathedral in Washington, D.C., attended our 1985 trip to Central America. Through him, I met Bishop John Walker, the first African American bishop of the Episcopal Church in Washington and a crusader against racial discrimination. Bishop Walker invited me to lead a three-day conference on Central America for approximately 120 priests and church leaders from the D.C. area. This was an ideal opportunity to inform church leaders in the nation's capital about the realities in Central America.

In 1983, following our first trip to Nicaragua, Gretchen and I decided to visit my family in Mexico City for a few days. Gretchen was delighted to spend time with them. She said my family had been so good to her that being with them made her feel that nothing could ever go wrong in the world.

Since she had heard me tell stories about living in the Mexico City tenement after my parents separated, she asked to see where we had lived. I took her there. We walked up three long flights of stairs. I could tell by her face that she was shocked. Perhaps she was trying to reconcile the place where she had grown up, in the countryside outside of Houston, with our ugly, tiny two-room apartment on Serapio Rendón Street in Mexico City.

After spending two days with my family, we said goodbye at the airport. Later that night, when we spoke by phone, Gretchen told me she had been so overcome that she missed her plane to Austin.

I wondered if she might be falling in love, as I was. Despite my feelings, she was hesitant to have a more intimate relationship, not only because of our pasts but because of her children.

CHAPTER THIRTEEN

A Glimpse of Paradise

*Good Adventure to you who
look for truth with singleness of heart:
you shall see God.*

—Jorge Lara-Braud, "Óscar
Romero: Beatitude Made Flesh"

Soon after returning from Nicaragua in 1983, I was given some vacation time. I agreed with Gretchen that I should use my time off to work with Pat Malone, a psychologist in Atlanta. I didn't want to enter another relationship and fail again. I also wanted Gretchen to have the confidence in me that I would succeed this time. Never before had I allowed myself the opportunity to stop and reflect. I had never faced my "shadow side"—the parts of me I had kept hidden. My aim was to do that now, so it would not continue to hurt me and those I loved. Pat also helped me understand how low self-esteem had led me to a pattern of compulsive overachieving.

Self-compassion, Pat emphasized, would help me to be more compassionate toward others. Thanks to him, I began to realize that although my childhood flight had been impetuous, it had also been positive. If I had not dared to leave Mamá, Luis, and Cachuy when I was a teenager, my life would have been severely limited. Attending Tex-Mex, joining the Presbyterian Church, learning to speak English, becoming a scholar and student leader—all had prepared and enabled me not only to assume positions of church leadership, but to become a fully mature human being.

Even though I was excelling in my career, I felt like a failure as a father. Pat encouraged me to be hopeful for a future relationship, although he understood it would be difficult.

Until I met Gretchen, there had been a separation between my private and public lives—as if there were an iron curtain between the two. Now I had an opportunity to merge them. Because

Gretchen had similar passions, I hoped I would not have such a struggle as before.[187]

Having spent those action-filled days in Nicaragua, now we had a chance to reflect and meditate. It occurred to me that, although apart, we could both do this together. In a letter, I proposed we focus together on the lectionary readings from the Book of Common Prayer.[188]

One reading from Joshua 4:19–5:1 tells how Joshua, who had taken Moses's place, led the Israelites across the Jordan River. Like the crossing of the Red Sea, years earlier, the waters of the Jordan parted allowing the twelve tribes of Israel, approximately 49,000 people, to enter the promised land. To commemorate their victorious crossing, Joshua asked each leader from the twelve tribes to place one stone on the land where they had entered.

I was inspired by the way the Israelites had met their challenges. In the same way, I wanted Gretchen and me to commemorate special moments in our short history. That's why I wrote to her and suggested we remember times like planting a redbud tree next to her back porch, our evening conversation while sitting on that boulder in the Jalapa schoolyard, and our time together at the airport in Mexico City before we said goodbye. These landmarks were, in my mind, like Ebenezers—stones of help, based on Samuel 7—the equivalent of crossing over to another stage of our lives onto solid ground.[189] I felt these remembrances could encourage us when facing future obstacles. As I wrote to Gretchen: "It is such a joy, even during a fragmented afternoon, to know we are now reflecting together on these ancient truths, so full of contemporary and future meaning."[190]

For love to last, we both knew, there needed to be more than a romantic attraction. I dared to believe we had that "more." During our trip to Nicaragua, we saw how we had already begun to make a unique difference not only for ourselves but for others as well. I had been inspired to confront my inner demons, and Gretchen was becoming more peaceful and hopeful.[191]

That December of 1983 I flew to Austin. Gretchen, Greta, and I then drove to San Miguel de Allende, Mexico, via Laredo and Saltillo.[192] Greta and I took turns driving while Gretchen wrote Christmas cards. Gretchen's father, Tom Shartle, met us in San Miguel. Understandably, he was a bit distant with me, probably wondering how serious Gretchen and I were about each other. Even so, it was good to see how warm he was with both Gretchen and Greta, and I looked forward to knowing him better.

From San Miguel, I took a bus to Mexico City to spend Christmas with my family. It was a special blessing to spend some quiet time alone with Mamá, and a joy to be with Cachuy, her husband, Jorge Espino, and their children. Little did I know this would be the last time I would see Mamá. One month later, Cachuy called me in tears to say that Mamá had died suddenly of a heart attack. Though very sad, I felt grateful to have seen her over Christmas.

It had been fourteen years since I had seen Jorge Luis, so long that I was beginning to give up on ever being together with him again. While I expected he might be at the funeral, seeing him there still surprised me. If I was nervous, I knew he must be feeling more so. None of my family had met his wife, Ida Cecilia. We embraced rather hesitantly. Later he said he did not recognize me because I had aged more than his mother or Cachuy. During the week following the funeral, we saw each other a few times at Cachuy's home. I was grateful we had begun to reconnect, and for the first time in years, I started to feel hopeful about our relationship.

That spring, I was beginning to experience the joy of family in other ways as well. Several times I traveled to Austin to be with Gretchen and Greta. During one of my visits in early March, I awakened with a sliver of a dream that seemed to be coming true. In the dream, it's a radiant morning in Gretchen's home. She and I are luxuriating in the loveliness of the moment. Unannounced and bouncing, a joyful Greta hugs us, then gets between us and asks us to hug her back, because she is delighted at the way our lives have come together.[193]

Although reading Scripture as well as keeping in touch by telephone and letters helped ground me during our times apart, I was impatient to be with Gretchen more permanently—that is, as her husband. I knew she loved me, yet she was also committed to her children—both Kyria, who had just graduated from high school in Virginia, and Greta, who was a sophomore at St. Stephen's Episcopal School in Austin. Gretchen was clear that she planned to wait three years, until after Greta had graduated from St. Stephen's, before marrying.

That felt like such a long time. My inclination was to pressure her to move faster, but deep down I knew that would not help. Once again, I found comfort in the Psalms, particularly the last verse of Psalm 33, which I cited in a letter to her: "Yahweh, let your love rest on us as our hope has rested in you."[194] Though at times afraid, in my heart I knew our lives would eventually come together. During one of those periods of knowing, I wrote to Gretchen: "My soul is singing again. I am centered. It is not something I am doing. It is not something you are doing. God should be pleased that we suspect He is responsible."[195]

In my effort to plan our future together, I inquired about the possibility of a teaching position at the Austin Presbyterian

Seminary. Unfortunately, that did not work out, but soon after, San Francisco Theological Seminary invited me to become professor of theology and culture, beginning in September 1984. Although I'd be even farther from Texas, this was an enticing opportunity, so I accepted the offer.

Even though I had pressured Gretchen for years to marry me, when Greta became a senior at St. Stephen's, we both hesitated. I was afraid of being tied down, and Gretchen was feeling cautious. Judith Liro, Gretchen's dearest friend in Austin, and Howard Rice, my very dear friend at the San Francisco seminary, counseled us to remember that a true marriage cannot happen without God. Howard emphasized that marriage can be a miraculously positive event, but also required courage. Both told us it would be wrong to remain single out of fear. Knowing us well, they counseled us to act audaciously and trust the love we felt for each other.

On June 16, 1986, one week after Greta graduated from high school, Gretchen and I married in her Austin home. Our favorite mariachis, the Romanceros, played. Judith Liro, an Episcopal priest, officiated. My sister and her husband attended along with their daughters, Silvia and Martha, and Martha's husband, Ramiro. Gretchen's father also joined us. And of course, Greta and Kyria were there. At the end of the ceremony, five ministers—one Catholic, one Lutheran, two Presbyterian, and one Episcopalian—all laid their hands on us while Judith led them in prayer. After we were blessed, the mariachis began to play and we broke out into dancing.[196]

As we make our vows, five ministers bless us.

We break out into dancing.

My sister, Cachuy, and her husband, Jorge Espino Arias

Soon after our guests left that evening, the telephone rang. An official from the World Council of Churches in Geneva was calling. He summoned me to El Salvador the next day to join others in negotiations with President José Napoleón Duarte and other Salvadoran government leaders. A few days before, fifteen Salvadoran church activists had been jailed. It was alleged that they had been bringing food, medicine, and weapons to Salvadoran insurgents. At first, I hesitated, fearing I might upset Gretchen, as this was not how I anticipated starting our marriage. But Gretchen urged me to go, saying she felt honored to participate even indirectly in something so close to her heart.[197] This was a good omen. Our marriage was starting with my career demanding my attention, but for once I had the support of my wife, who saw the importance of my work.

A GLIMPSE OF PARADISE

Jorge negotiating with President Duarte in San Salvador

Three of us met with President Duarte in San Salvador. We made it very clear to him that the eyes of the world were on him and El Salvador. Countless church leaders throughout the world would hold him responsible if a single church activist was further detained or hurt. The following day, we were relieved when President Duarte freed all fifteen prisoners.

Gretchen met me at the airport in Houston, and we drove together to Crockett in East Texas for a meeting with her family. In many ways, this was harder than my meeting with President Duarte. Gretchen had warned me that her brother and sister would probably have little interest in my trip. Even so, it was a blow when they responded so negatively to my accounts. They knew nothing about the conflicts in Central America and did not care to learn. Gretchen was accustomed to their indifference, so it did not surprise her, but still it saddened her.

That summer, we decided to take a break from Central America and spend some time in France. We planned our time in France around Greta, who would be living with a French family in Avignon. Gretchen and I helped Greta move into the home of Madame Augier. I loved being involved with those kinds of familial tasks. While proficient in Spanish, Greta was struggling with French. When Madame Augier asked her if she slept well, Greta thought that meant, hurry and take a shower! Most days after class, Greta would zip over to the inn where we were staying, have lunch with us, then join us for an afternoon rest.

I wished I could speak better French. Soon after our arrival, I surprised Gretchen while listening to the news. The radio on my Walkman was broadcasting in English. With the headphones on I said to Gretchen, "Look, I can translate the news from French into English!" I did not miss a cue and Gretchen thought I was actually translating. Later, I revealed my secret and the three of us had a good laugh.

Once Greta was settled in Avignon, Gretchen and I left to explore the countryside. The rhythm of our days was easy and relaxed, like the flowers and dry grasses in Lagarrigue and Venasque. A week later, we returned to Avignon to meet up with Greta and drive north through the Alps to Alsace. Gretchen was glad, because it meant she could introduce Greta and me to her French family in Strasbourg, where she had spent the summer of 1955. Her French father, Monsieur Ditner, said that for him seeing us was the "*bonheur de cette année*" (the happiness of that year). Madame Ditner liked me and was glad to see her American daughter was happily finding her way. Our time with them made me feel even more a part of my own new family.[198]

Madame Ditner, Gretchen, and Monsieur Ditner in Strasbourg, 1986

Soon after we arrived, I learned that the Ditners' Protestant pastor was Dr. Miguel Ángel Brun. In 1972, Brun had been incarcerated by the Uruguayan right-wing military government. He had spent eighteen months in the penitentiary, where he was tortured numerous times with a cattle prod. His torturers had been determined to get information about others in opposition to the government. Though tortured for days, he refused to talk. This was the first time we had actually met, but I had in fact worked for months to free him and his wife from prison when I was at the National Council of Churches. It was very gratifying to finally meet him and to realize I had played a small role in his release.

At the end of the summer, all three of us flew back to California. Greta would begin her studies at Scripps College in Claremont, California, that fall, and we would be living on the seminary campus in San Anselmo, north of San Francisco. Dean Walt Davis and his wife, Libby, lived just across the street. Randy Taylor, our seminary president, lived in a lovely mansion halfway up seminary hill.

Randy and I had become friends years before when we worked on bringing the Northern and Southern Presbyterian Churches together.[199] My beloved friend, Howard Rice, also lived nearby. In many ways, it was an ideal community setting.

In addition to our friends on the faculty, right away Gretchen and I connected with some of my students, especially Tim Lanham and his wife, Gigi, from Montana. Tim missed the wildness of the land in Montana and used to say, "The problem with Marin [County] is that it is imbued with terminal cuteness." Tim was in the small group that I led called Exploration in Ministry. To earn money for his tuition, Tim worked for the seminary doing landscaping. After he cut our grass, Gretchen often invited Tim to join us for lunch and conversation about our lives and God. Once he brought a paper he had written for class. Tim rather liked it when Gretchen told him frankly she found his paper a bit boring—even "highfalutin." He later said that this made him think, "Am I writing for myself or for pointy-headed academics?"[200]

When we came back from Europe that August, we were greeted not only by a special sense of community at the seminary, but by letters from Cachuy. She began by saying how much she had loved being with us at our wedding, "Never have I experienced such a happy time with you in your country."[201] Cachuy was happy, feeling that at last I had found peace in my life. Cachuy even dared to give Gretchen bits of sisterly advice. She told her we would both be happier if only Gretchen could "*matar el gallo de Jorge*," which means "to kill my rooster" or "tame my cockiness." I felt blessed myself that the budding spirit of affection between Gretchen and Cachuy began a weaving of *cariño* (love) embracing everyone in my family.[202]

A GLIMPSE OF PARADISE

As I read the news and received the love Cachuy sent us, I felt glad, but also sad to be so far away. I was proud of my son, nieces, and nephews who were going forward in their lives. I so wished we could find a way to simultaneously be at San Francisco Theological Seminary and in Mexico City. Cachuy ended all of her letters saying, "receive the *cariño* from your family who loves you."

Some of our best times while in California were spent at Skyline Ranch, a property to the north of Marin County that belonged to the family of one of my seminary students, Diane Pendola. Each year, Diane and her partner, Teresa Hahn, invited two women about to be sentenced to prison to live there with them. After spending time with Diana and Teresa at Skyline, these women would often have their jail terms reduced by two years. During the day, I used to join the women clearing brush and cutting wood for making fences and building fires. I usually came in from work just in time for lunch, with my pants and boots muddy, exclaiming about the beauties of the simple life. During one of those visits, Gretchen wrote to Cachuy:

> Here comes my Jorge with two women from the jail who have been struggling with alcoholism. Surely they will all be hungry! I see his smile from far away! Oo la la how wonderful to be with my husband who is so very happy![203]

In the evenings, we would read a piece from Alcoholics Anonymous. Afterward, we'd sit together meditating for more than thirty minutes. Then, each of us would talk about our struggles and joys of that day.

After one of our trips to Skyline, we had a large fiesta to welcome Jorge Luis, his wife, and my new granddaughter, Gina. This was the first time I had laid eyes on her, and I was overjoyed to hold her. Gretchen had found a man from Mexico who played mariachi music. A friend of Kyria's came up from San Francisco to cook Mexican food. I knew our dancing would probably flow from inside the house out into the garden. Dancing together with family, friends, students, and colleagues to the rhythm of mariachis was a joy.

Jorge and Gretchen at a San Anselmo fiesta

My focus, of course, was on my teaching and my students. Tim Lanham once told me:

> My other seminary professors taught me to think about the Bible, theology, and ethics. But you helped me think

about life and, in the process, to love it on a fundamental level. So when I see how many people live and die without ever loving life, I appreciate even more the gift of the perspective you helped nurture inside of me.[204]

Later he also said how much he appreciated that I encouraged him to be "down to earth," to know that the practice of theology is never done in an ivory tower—but rather within the context of life where we are called to live and be faithful. Having students like Tim kept me aware that my work was worthwhile. Years later, he said I was precisely the "right person, at the right place and the right time for him."[205]

The following year, two more of my students, Janet Riley and John Lersch, joined the Circle of Refuge, a student group I had created to focus on Central America. I repeatedly encouraged students in that group to find ways to live their faith. We visited a deportation center in Southern California called El Centro, then raised bail for Mexican and Central American detainees. We also went to the Concord Naval Weapons Station to protest weapons being sent to the Contras in Honduras. Years later, Janet told me it was partly because of their participation in the Circle of Refuge that she and John became attracted to one another and married. Later they had triplets.

Circle of Refuge group, May 1985, San Anselmo, California

Back row—Tim Lanham, Gretchen, Chuck, Gigi Lanham, and Ron. Middle—Woodley, Lynn, and Jackie. Front—Mary, Jorge, and Karie

Circle of Refuge at a seminary retreat

A GLIMPSE OF PARADISE

So many aspects of our seminary life had the glow of paradise. From the beginning, I was challenged in my teaching. I had been chosen as Professor of the Year for the seminary in 1989, and that same year I was asked to give the baccalaureate address for Stanford University. In some ways, it seemed too good to be true.

1989 baccalaureate address at Stanford University

Then on October 17, 1989, an earthquake hit Northern California leaving death and destruction in its wake. Shortly thereafter, Gretchen and I felt the foundations of our marriage had also been shaken. Out of respect for the intimacy of our love, I will not reveal the details. Gretchen moved back to Austin so we could have some time apart.

During the next year, through our own determination, the encouragement of friends, and hard work with an expert counselor, we first faced our difficulties alone, then, later, together. Most importantly, we forgave one another and moved on to a more peaceful stage in our lives.

CHAPTER FOURTEEN

Can We Believe in God after This?

Thank God, this is a wounded God.
Not almighty in power, but almighty in love.
And because love never dies,
death will be conquered.

—Jorge Lara-Braud, "1492–1992: Can We Believe in God after This?"

While still raw from the trauma, I began to ask the question, "Can we believe in God after this?" I eventually moved back into the Austin home with Gretchen during the summer of 1990. Soon after that, I became a visiting scholar at the Institute of Latin American Studies at the University of Texas, which gave me access to the Benson Latin American Collection, one of the top Latin American libraries in the world. Consequently, when Jack Stotts, the president of the Austin Presbyterian Theological Seminary, invited me to be the sole speaker for the 1992 Settles Lectures that fall, I felt confident. The subject of my presentation would be the legacy of Columbus five hundred years after his landing in the New World, and there was no better place in the world to do the research for this topic than the Benson.[206]

Jack Stotts playing charades at an Expanding Horizons board retreat in 2006

The subject of Columbus connected with my passion to stand up for oppressed people. Before beginning my research, I already knew that many Native Americans had died directly, and indirectly, as a result of Columbus's and other explorers' expeditions to the New World. However, I was horrified to discover the vastness of the devastation. Between 1492 and 1650, the population of the Caribbean Islands, Central America, Mexico, and Peru dropped from approximately 50 million to around 5 million people, a loss of about 90 percent.[207]

That so many deaths occurred was a horror, but almost worse, the enterprises were covered with a religious veil legitimized by Catholic monarchs and four papal bulls (signed by Pope Alexander VI in 1493). The entire endeavor encompassing several expeditions was seen in a holy light, because efforts were made to baptize the natives into the Christian faith. Also, in the name of holiness the sacred lives of those natives were stripped away. They lost not only their physical lives but their very souls.

The fact that Columbus's expedition, and following ones, were made to appear so closely associated with God led to a justification of actions that have become inhuman practices for a great deal of subsequent history. Thus began a habitual pattern of denigrating darker-skinned people, a practice that continues to this day.

Long before I prepared this presentation on Columbus, the suffering in this world and how God could allow it perplexed me. The number of innocent Jewish people who died in the Holocaust, the enslavement of Africans in the Americas, and the numerous innocent people in Central America heartlessly killed—how could God have allowed so much suffering to occur?

At the end of my presentation, the question I asked was whether we could possibly believe in God after learning about these atrocities. Indeed, if God is all-powerful, why didn't God prevent such horrors? I had always struggled with these questions, but now for the first time I felt pressed to find answers. I began to wonder if God was actually all-powerful, and concluded that God too was suffering.

We must be prepared to believe that in some mysterious way God has experienced every unjust death, with agony and screams reverberating from here to eternity in the infinity of God's self. *Thank God, this is a wounded God, not almighty in power, but almighty in love; and because love never dies, death will be conquered.*[208]

Realizing these deaths were not allowed by an all-powerful God helped me be closer to God. Even so, my research and the conclusions I had drawn from it left me shaken to the point of questioning the strength of my own faith.

That same year came a surprise that restored my soul. A small Presbyterian congregation located a few blocks east of I-35 in East Austin, El Buen Pastor Presbyterian Church, asked me to consider serving as their pastor. That experience would open up possibilities for me to serve my community and beyond in ways none of us could have previously imagined. I had always been attracted to El Buen Pastor because it was in the heart of Austin's Mexican American community. Even so, I had never envisioned serving as its pastor.

This opportunity arose when I was invited to preach the homily at the funeral of a saintly matriarch of the church who died in the fall of 1992. Before the evening was over, the church elders were asking me to take charge of the preaching on Sundays. I agreed to do so thinking the assignment would be temporary.[209] Serving at El Buen Pastor became a blessing—a way to serve others and to grow myself. I found joy transitioning from my role as a theologian in the seminary to an active position as a parish pastor. While talking about the gospel had been meaningful, bringing the precepts to life was far more powerful.

El Buen Pastor Presbyterian Church at the corner of Waller and Willow Streets

Photo by Isabella Knight, May 2022

My biggest challenge was language. For at least half of the people, English was their language of choice. This group required a substantial amount of English in every part of the liturgy, especially in the sermon. The other half, who ranged from near-bilingual to Spanish monolingual, expected Spanish to be the primary language for everything. However, the Spanish they spoke was not what one hears in Mexico or elsewhere in Latin America. It was a patois that sounds like Spanish but relies heavily on borrowings from English prefixes, suffixes, and sentence structure, all in a mix that creates hundreds of new words and expressions.

How do you pray with or preach to such a diversity of congregants? My own approach was a constant improvisation that paradoxically required a great deal of preparation to make it seem spontaneous. I followed the Sunday Bible readings of the international liturgical calendar and provided the lay readers with the simplest possible translations in both languages. I wrote out the homilies in Spanish, making sure everything was simple, correct, and natural, with a touch of poetry here and there. I taped what I had written, then memorized it as much as possible by listening to it a number of times on the last two days of the week, and finally once more on Sunday en route to church. When I delivered it, I had nothing in my hands. I would step away from the pulpit and stand at the edge of the chancel closest to the first pew. Then, in a way that was virtually conversational, I proceeded to preach in sequences composed of a few lines in one language followed by a slightly briefer version of those lines in the other language, sometimes letting the second language of the last sequence become the first language of the next. I also printed the homilies in English and Spanish so people could follow in both languages. It appeared that everyone understood.[210]

After a few months, parishioners began encouraging me to serve them on a more permanent basis. By the beginning of 1993, I realized I wanted to become the commissioned lay preacher of El Buen Pastor. Right away, I knew this would be challenging because of my decision in 1956 not to become ordained. This choice had made sense back then, when I was planning to live and work in Mexico, because Protestant ministers and Catholic priests in Mexico were not allowed to vote or speak out about political issues. Because I had completed all the courses necessary for ordination and had even taught many of them, I first applied to the local presbytery, or governing body of the Presbyterian Church, hoping to be ordained quickly. I also contacted my friend Jim Andrews, the Stated Clerk of the General Assembly of the Presbyterian Church, asking for his advice and counsel. I felt reassured when he ascertained there would be no problem. However, the process took over a year and was more complicated than either he or I had foreseen.

Although not ordained, I was finally installed as lay pastor on September 11, 1994. What a lively occasion that was! About six hundred people from near and far, from every walk of life, came to be with us. It was inspiring to see so many faces of the Christ we are called to serve.

Jorge and Gretchen on the day of his installation as lay pastor of El Buen Pastor Presbyterian Church in Austin, Texas

Soon after I was installed, my son Jorge Luis, who was then working for Kodak in Mexico, came for a visit. I invited him to read the Scripture and direct the service while I preached. It was customary to invite a church member to play this role. No doubt, I am biased, but I do not know of anyone else who can read more clearly in Spanish and English, or direct the service more professionally, than he. Afterward, Nery Gonzales, one of my parishioners from Chiapas, echoed my views: "Your son spoke Spanish and English so eloquently, his style so smooth, not unlike yours." Of course, I felt proud.

In my first year as a minister, we received a total of twenty new members: six from Mexico, one from Guatemala, and the other twelve from different parts of the United States, including one African American, six Anglos, and five Mexican Americans. Among these new members were people who had very few years of schooling in either Spanish or English. Most of them were earning their living as manual laborers or service workers. At the other end were professionals who possessed one, two, or three university degrees, all of whom had invested their lives in some kind of humanitarian work.[211]

Next to preaching, my highest joy as a pastor was the companionship of splendid colleagues like Raúl Gonzales, who administered with flair and faithfulness the ministries connected with El Buen Pastor. One such ministry, the El Buen Pastor Early Childhood Development Center, was adjacent to the church. Many of the poorest children in our community received their educational start there before going to public school. We also offered after-school tutorials and taught English as a second language. In another wing of the church, Manos de Cristo (Hands of Christ) encompassed a dental clinic, a food pantry, and a used-clothes "closet." How gratifying it was to hear so many people referring to our Presbyterian corner of Waller and Willow Streets as "*la esquina de compasión*" (the corner of compassion).[212]

Raúl Gonzales honoring Jorge during Sunday services—Linda Ruiz on the left

After church, people would often congregate outside the entrance on the "*esquina de compasión.*" Yet there was something unwelcoming—indeed, less than compassionate—about people gathering on a concrete sidewalk in the glaring hot sun. Some of our parishioners suggested we plant pistachio trees for shade. They also chose homemade bricks to replace the ugly concrete ones. More than thirty people paid forty dollars apiece to commemorate their deceased family members with an inscribed memorial brick located in the courtyard next to the church, which we named "*la Placita de los Santos*" (the place of the saints). Our own special ritual to commemorate "*la Placita de los Santos*" took place on May 20, 1996. We made a large circle around the courtyard and held hands as we prayed that our special friends in heaven would feel blessed by our prayers. After praying, we spoke the names of the people inscribed on the bricks. The bricks brightened after red and white flowers were placed on people's names. Included among the people inscribed on our special memorial bricks were not only parishioners from El Buen Pastor, but friends and family who lived far away.

Gretchen and Jorge laying flowers on the bricks at the *"esquina de compasión"* in the *"Placita de los Santos,"* May 27, 1997

CAN WE BELIEVE IN GOD AFTER THIS? 191

Mexican pistachio tree in the courtyard of El Buen Pastor Church

Photo by Isabella Knight, May 2022

Bricks in the *"Placita de los Santos"*

Part of my attraction to ritual came from growing up in the Catholic Church. Many Mexican Presbyterian churches steered away from rituals like Ash Wednesday. They were too close to the Catholic Church's practices. Recognizing this day at El Buen Pastor was my way of beginning to include some elements of Catholicism and attempting a reconciliation between the faiths, something I had struggled to achieve for most of my life. Few people in our church understood that the tendency toward anti-Catholicism on the part of some Americans was often an expression of Anglo prejudice against Hispanics and other minorities. Since the majority of Latinos in the United States are Catholics, it made no sense for the country's Hispanic Protestant churches to be anti-Catholic.

The first time we celebrated Ash Wednesday was in 1993. After serving sandwiches and bread pudding, traditional foods for Mexican people during Lent, we gathered in the church for a service. After the initial hymns, we all wrote one of our sins on a piece of paper. Then we put our papers in a bucket lined with aluminum foil and set them afire. Afterward, we put those ashes on our foreheads as we said in English or Spanish: "*Cenizas a las cenizas, de polvo al polvo*" (Ashes to ashes, dust to dust).

During that time, I initiated a weekly ritual as an integral part of our church service. After the sermon, some people approached the communion table and knelt on surrounding cushions. I blessed each person kneeling by placing my hands gently on their heads in the spirit of lovingkindness. They would then whisper their need for forgiveness and healing to me. At the end, I gathered what people had told me. Without violating anyone's privacy, I stated their concerns to the whole congregation so we could all pray together for the struggles of others. For many of us, this simple ritual brought words from the gospel like love and forgiveness to life.

CAN WE BELIEVE IN GOD AFTER THIS?

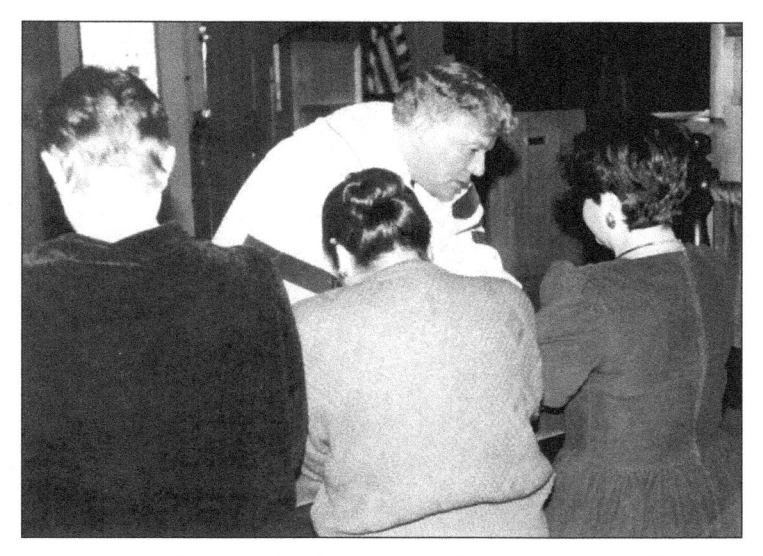

Jorge blessing parishioners at El Buen Pastor Church

While teaching at seminary, I had often felt removed from the gospel; now, working in the barrio, I was living it. There was a drug rehabilitation center just around the corner from El Buen Pastor. I made friends with the director, then invited those in rehabilitation to attend our services. They came that next Sunday and sat sheepishly on the back row. When I noticed the men from the center, I stopped our service and invited them to come to the front. After that, they came many times, and I always insisted they sit in front.

Front page, *Austin American-Statesman*, Easter Sunday, March 30, 1997[213]

Gretchen handing out flowers to welcome the men from Remar, a drug rehabilitation center

During the week, I was sometimes surprised by people who knocked on my office door. Once a boy around fifteen years old arrived. He reminded me of myself when I left home. Having heard about me and El Buen Pastor Church in El Salvador, he walked north from El Salvador through Mexico, all the way to Austin. He planned to go on to his aunt in New York City. After this young man had rested and eaten, I bought him a bus ticket and sent him on his way to be reunited with his aunt.

One day people from a local nursing home phoned me to say one of my parishioners was close to death and requested that I come. When I arrived, the doctor told me she had just died, so there was no reason to go into her room. I insisted and asked that I be left alone with her for a few minutes. During those minutes, I prayed. To my surprise she began to breathe. The doctor was amazed to find she was alive. She returned to El Buen Pastor after two weeks and continued coming to church for several months until she finally died.

While at El Buen Pastor, I had other experiences that confirmed the adage "Expect the unexpected!" One involved my budding friendship with Gretchen's father, Tom Shartle. Before I began my teaching job at San Francisco Theological Seminary in 1984, we barely knew each other. He and I came from two different worlds: he from the world of commerce and industry, I from the world of religion and academia. He was a solid American; I, a Mexican immigrant. For those reasons, people thought Tom and I would never become friends.

During the early 1990s when I was serving as pastor of El Buen Pastor, he and I slowly became closer. Every three weeks or so, Gretchen and I would drive to East Texas mainly to be with Tom at his cattle ranch in the pines. Tom was eighty-four, still lucid, though something of an invalid.[214] Later, as I got to know him better, I used to drive to Crockett by myself. I came to enjoy being with him alone when Gretchen was away on trips. We'd drive together to see the ducks on the pond near the ranch house, then check out the lake and drive through the pine forest.

Gretchen, Tom, and Jorge at Hickory Creek Ranch in East Texas

Sometime after Tom died, I realized he had given me the chance to befriend, and actually love, someone quite different from myself. Not unlike the themes of many gospel stories, my experience with Tom showed how we can open our hearts and allow love to jump over conventional boundaries. His natural kindness allowed the lines that differentiated us to blur. I felt more at ease with him than with my own father, and far more than I had with Ruth's dad, Señor Marroquín. I often joked with Tom, one time predicting that Jesse Jackson would become president of the United States. Tom responded, "Yeah, yeah, then we'll all be on welfare."

But he would say these things in such a devilish way that I couldn't stop myself from laughing and responding, "Tom, there is no hope for you." Then he would laugh and say something like, "There is hope for me, because you have good connections 'upstairs,' and I'm sure you will persuade them to forgive me." While Tom was often humorous and exuberant, he was also reserved. Consequently, I was surprised when one day he said to Gretchen, "You know, I really do love Jorge."

A few years before he died, he asked that I be the one to conduct his memorial service. Increasingly, I found there was no fixed line between my family life and my service as a pastor. Although Tom was not a member of El Buen Pastor, he was a dear member of my family, so I felt honored to accept his request.

In December 1996, when we visited Tom in the Crockett Hospital, we knew he was in a struggle for his life. But we prayed he would live at least until mid-January after our return from our planned weeklong family vacation at Rancho la Puerta near Tijuana, Mexico. However, on Gretchen's sixtieth birthday, January 10, the phone rang in our San Diego hotel room. It was Gretchen's brother Charles calling to say Tom had just died. Since Tom had chosen to be cremated, Charles agreed to wait until the following week to have the memorial service, which would take place in Crockett soon after our return from Tijuana.

Even though we were at this lovely place walking, exercising, and exploring, our thoughts were often focused on Tom. "Dad died... granddaddy is gone... uncle Tom has died." Gretchen and I thought it would be comforting to have a special gathering while we were at Rancho la Puerta. We gathered together with cousins, from Tom's brother's family, on a sunny spot of green grass. Cousin Sarah led us in a recitation of the Twenty-Third Psalm.

I read Revelation 21 about the meeting of a new heaven and a new earth, a place where there will be no tears, where everyone will have enough. I mentioned how I always felt so welcomed by Tom, how he made everyone feel at home, even those who spoke no English. My voice cracked with emotion when I expressed how much I loved him. Gretchen's daughter Kyria also began to cry during our informal ceremony. Our cousin Weezie Coleman comforted her. As we walked back afterward, I told Gretchen that Kyria brought feeling into the service.

After that healing week together in Mexico, Kyria, Gretchen, and I went to Austin, where I focused on the memorial service, which would take place in Crockett. Greta had flown in from London, where she was living, while others were driving up from Houston. A particular challenge for me personally was to speak sincerely from my heart about Tom's death without being too sentimental because of how much I loved him.

Before the memorial service, we buried the urn containing Tom's ashes in a muddy hole. Rain was pouring down. Many were standing beneath a few umbrellas. The fact that we shared umbrellas—that everyone found a place to stand beneath one—made me think of the loaves-and-fishes experience in the Bible. Greta sheltered me as I read from the Book of Common Prayer. As we were leaving the cemetery, the clouds opened and out sprang a rainbow.

After the burial, we held a service at First United Methodist Church of Crockett. I began by telling a memory, recently recalled. Gretchen and I had gone to the ranch in Crockett to spend a few days with Tom. He and I were in the small sitting room. I was reading; he was in his recliner—at times dozing off, at times looking distantly, as if chasing some intriguing reverie. Something startled him. He turned to me and asked anxiously for his wife, "Jorge, where is Ruth?" (Gretchen's mother).

I replied, "Ruth is in heaven, Tom."

With a sigh of relief, he murmured, "Then, all is well."

"Yes," I agreed, "all is well." He then closed his eyes, his face bathed in serenity.

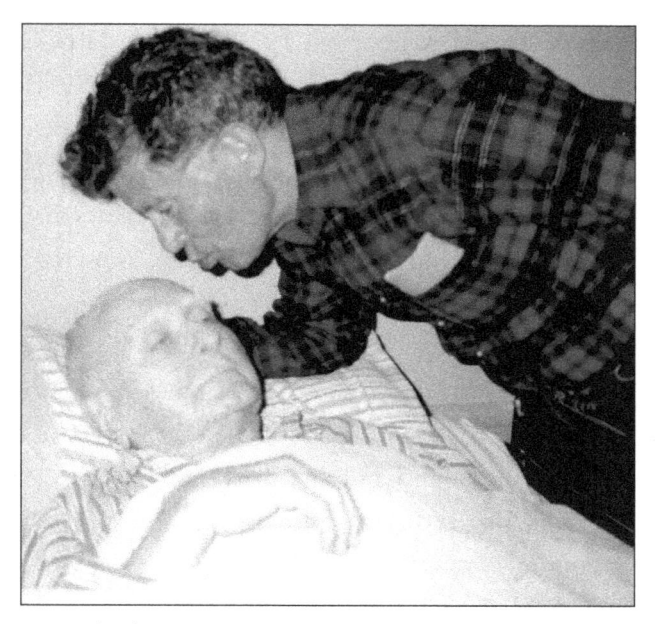

Jorge kissing Tom a few months before his death

These comments opened the way for me to speak of the resurrection. Since we had just put his ashes into the earth next to his wife's, I spoke of our bodies being returned to dust—surely, we have not been brought forth from the dust to be returned to dust forever. What a cruel joke that would be. Surely, the God who made us from the dust is quite capable of remaking us from the dust. Surely, the God who made us to be his companions will accompany us to the place where "Death will be no more; mourning and crying and pain will be no more."[215] Christian faith is sustained by the certainty of the resurrection. That certainty allowed us to speak that afternoon of Tom as one who had lived and as one who would live again.[216]

A representative from the Salvation Army spoke movingly of Tom's contributions to that organization. Apparently, Tom had raised one million dollars when he served as chairman of the board of the Salvation Army from 1970 to 1974. How could he have kept that a secret from us for so many years, all the while joking with Gretchen and me about being "do-gooders"?

Tom's death made me feel more committed than ever before to life. I had recently been diagnosed with Parkinson's disease and wanted to give all I could to those around me, knowing I might not have long to live myself.

Focusing on the gospel in preaching motivated me to reach out to people beyond El Buen Pastor who were struggling. Consequently, when Laura Mendenhall, the pastor of Austin's Westminster Presbyterian Church, called in November 1994 asking me for help, I agreed. Her church wanted to give $2,500 to deserving families.

Members of El Buen Pastor had come to know extremely needy families from their work with the Early Childhood Development Center and Manos de Cristo. Together we identified fourteen needy families. To protect the dignity of the recipients, I decided to go alone to visit them. Besides money, what the poor need is the opportunity to be understood and say what they hoped for.

Among those I spoke with was a woman whom I shall call Doña Lencha and her son, Fernandito. Two years before, her husband had left her and her three children, when they were living in a rural community in southern Mexico. When poverty got so extreme that it threatened to destroy her and her family, she came to Austin with her children. She had hoped that by working as a domestic, she could support herself and her family. However, since her arrival a year before, she had been too ill to work.

Doña Lencha and her friend Carmelita received me courteously but with some embarrassment. It was a two-room apartment with just a hint of heat, and almost totally bare, except for two rickety chairs and a tattered couch covered with a lumpy blanket. Doña Lencha began to remove the blanket, I thought to create enough space for me to sit. To my amazement, she reached underneath and brought out in her arms a hefty boy who woke up smiling and making a noise I could not decipher.

She told me about the child, Fernandito, who was actually thirteen years old. Soon after their arrival in the United States, Doña Lencha had allowed Fernandito to attend a fiesta in East Austin. Unbeknownst to her, the young man who drove him was just learning to drive and did not have a license. Later that night, word came to Doña Lencha that Fernandito was in a local hospital fighting for his life. Fernandito and the driver had been in a head-on collision in which the young driver was killed. Fernandito was in a coma. When he awoke after two and a half months, his brain was severely damaged and the rest of his body was badly hurt.

While Doña Lencha was telling me the story, Fernandito's two younger brothers and Carmelita had formed a circle sitting on the floor. They looked spellbound. Fernandito was seated next to me, leaning hard on the back of the couch to remain upright. He seemed truly pleased, so pleased he kept on flashing me charming smiles, while running his unsteady fingers up and down my face. I smiled back and hugged him.

My emotions almost led me to forget the reason for my visit. I wiped my eyes, cleared my throat, reached inside my coat for the two envelopes, and began to explain. I told them that the envelope contained a gift from an anonymous Christian who wanted children to have a happy Christmas and to remember the best gift of all, the gift of "*el Niño Dios*" (the Godchild).

Doña Lencha reached inside the envelope and began with a look of delight to extract one bill at a time. Just then Fernandito, who since the accident had not succeeded in saying more than an isolated word here or there, said with astonishing clarity, "*¡Mami, Mami, dinero: lo que no tenemos!*" (Mommy, Mommy, money: what we do not have!) And then he beamed. He was so proud of himself. He must have known he had crossed the boundary from impossibility to possibility.

Doña Lencha shouted to no one in particular, "*¿Lo oyeron? ¿Lo oyeron? ¡Habló, habló!*" (Did you hear him? Did you hear him? He talked! He talked!)

Then she stood Fernandito up. We stood with him. From somewhere, the boy gathered strength to reach around his mother's waist and did the same thing with me with the other hand; then, with greater strength still, he forced us to place our cheeks against his, and shouted loudly to me, "*¡Rece, pastor, rece!*" (Pray, pastor, pray!).

Of course, I did, and wonder of wonders, he began to repeat perfectly everything he heard me say, and kept it up until I finished. At that point, Doña Lencha let go. I held on to Fernandito. She went down on her knees and in a loud voice thanked God and the Virgin of Guadalupe for the miracle we had witnessed.

It was time for me to go. There was no need to say any more. In fact, there was a kind of reverential silence as I took my leave.

Something truly sacred had happened. Could it be that a gift given with no strings had let life loose?[217]

Experiences like this, with Fernandito and Doña Lencha, moved me to raise money for the El Buen Pastor Early Childhood Development Center. Our excellent director, Linda Ruiz, and six teachers served fifty needy children. They were all packed into three small rooms in a ramshackle house next to the church. Seeing the children day after day, in that crowded environment, had moved me to help.

Linda Ruiz and Jorge in the courtyard of El Buen Pastor among the children of the Early Childhood Development Center

With the children in mind, I met with Paul Hilgers, who was then serving in the City of Austin's Neighborhood and Community Development Department, and his father, Bill Hilgers, a top-notch lawyer and dear friend. I invited Paul and Bill to visit El Buen Pastor's Early Childhood Development Center so they could see the pressing need with their own eyes. After some research, Paul informed me that the rebuilding plans for the childcare center would indeed be eligible for a community development block grant funded by the U.S. Department of Housing and Urban Development. Linda Ruiz and her staff went to work on the grant application process, which had to be vetted by the Austin City Council. Bill did the necessary legal work. My friend City Councilman Gus García helped us persuade his fellow council members to support the application.

We contacted individuals, prayer groups, and churches around the city to pray. More than once, Gretchen and I awakened at the same moment between three and four in the morning. We were surprised to learn we were both praying for the center. In our prayer group and at church, I joined others in what we called the "big prayer"—that the *"esquina de compasión"* might become a life-transforming source for many children in this Hispanic section of Austin.

The miracle occurred, just as it had for Fernandito. We were amazed to learn that on November 7, 1996, HUD would designate $1,122,000 to El Buen Pastor Early Childhood Development Center for the building of a new center. While HUD would provide the money to build the center, it was up to us to raise the funds to support it. The answer to the question I asked in the beginning—"Can we believe in God after this?"—was confirmed once again: "Yes, we can!"

CAN WE BELIEVE IN GOD AFTER THIS?

George W. Bush when he was governor visiting El Buen Pastor for the announcement of the HUD grant

Groundbreaking for the new center—
Linda Ruiz (middle shovel),
Bill Hilgers (far right)

CHAPTER FIFTEEN

Springs in the Desert

*The wilderness and the dry land shall be glad,
the desert shall rejoice and blossom;
like the crocus.*

—Isaiah 35:1 (NRSV)

In the spring of 2000, I underwent abdominal hernia surgery. We all hoped this would alleviate the increasingly severe abdominal pain from which I was suffering; instead, it exacerbated it. Gretchen and I believed that the pain was only made worse by the mesh the surgeon had placed in my abdomen after repairing the hernia.

Also, I was becoming increasingly debilitated from Parkinson's, with which I had been diagnosed in the mid-1990s. Gretchen and I believed my illness probably came from the water barrel dosed with Paraquat to kill mosquitos in Nicaragua. Paraquat is a known cause of the disease. To stop its progression, I hoped to see a highly regarded neurosurgeon in Mexico City. He planned to do a stem cell transplant into the part of the brain where critical cells were dying.

While awaiting treatment in Mexico City, I decided to go to a special clinic for healing in Tijuana in June of 2000. While there, I spent hours reaching out to others who were also in dire straits. I particularly focused on a seventeen-year-old who was fatally ill. The moment I returned to Austin, his parents called to say he had died. They asked me to conduct his funeral in Brenham, Texas. I left immediately. When Greta learned what was happening, she contacted me saying, "Jorge, you have been at this clinic for your own healing. Now you are back home. It is urgent for you to focus on your self for once!" But I did not listen.

I wrote a letter to friends describing my life with Parkinson's. I was having more trouble walking and remaining wakeful. I needed radical help. This degenerative disease was causing me more disability, indignity, and pain each day. My speech was now barely audible and quite tremulous. Sometimes, when I heard myself talk, it was like hearing a stranger trying so hard to achieve clarity of speech and thought that he ends up sounding frightened, apologetic, at a loss for words. That was not easy for me, especially since I had worked hard all my life to use words well.

Meanwhile, the tremors in various parts of my body were getting more severe. My legs, in particular, were increasingly unreliable. Understandably, I had to resign from every board, committee, task force, and commission in which I was involved.[218]

Among the responses to my letter, a special one came from Walter and June Keener Wink:

> We will be praying for the doctors to be inspired, brilliant, and on the money; for the nurses to be filled with healing virtue; for your body to respond to the treatment; for your family to be at peace and at rest; for you and Gretchen to sustain each other in faith and hope. We are pulling for you.
>
> Love,
>
> Walter and June.[219]

During the summer of 2000, while being attended by doctors in Mexico City, the highlight was visiting with my granddaughters, Gina and Melissa. Knowing I might live only a few more years, these times were especially precious. Fortunately for us, we would soon welcome another little one. On July 24, 2000, Clara, Kyria's daughter, and Gretchen's first grandchild, was born. I called Clara my "*nietecita*." Although she was a little young for a letter, I wrote to her from Mexico in September 2000:

Mi Muy Querida Nietecita,

I've been wanting to write you to let you know again how special you are. It isn't only that you're beautiful, or that you have such good lungs for singing (and crying). No, it's more than that. When you were born, you brought with you a chunk of heaven. Suddenly, all of us who were waiting for your arrival were no longer the same. You changed us all.

You confirmed with your landing that God does care for us, enough to give us a jewel like you; that his creation keeps on being surprising and awesome, like you; that to be your Mom, your Dad, your *Lita*, or your *Lito*, your *Tía*, your *Tío*, your aunt or your uncle, your friend or your helper is to touch and be touched by the heavenly one.

From your *Lito* who loves you dearly, Jorge[220]

Jorge with granddaughters Melissa (left) and Gina (right) in Mexico City

Jorge in the pool with Clara in Tucson, 2001

Much of what I undertook during those years drained me, but in contrast, working with my family was life-giving. In the fall of 2000, I worked with two close relatives during their marital struggle. I will call them "Julia" and "Paul." Julia later recounted this story to Jan Williams, a friend of Gretchen's.

> I wanted to leave my husband because of the errors he had committed. I was in despair. Jorge said that if there had been love in the relationship, and if there was still a little love left, then there was "*esperanza*," or hope.
>
> My husband doesn't easily express his feelings to others. But he talked so openly to Jorge that he cried.

My feelings of resentment kept me from healing quickly. It took a while. Jorge said, "Whatever happened, happened. Look forward, not back." Then each time I remembered what had happened, it would make me really furious. Jorge said to let it go, let it be. It was six months or so before I could begin to see our relationship as authentic again.

Without Jorge, we may have divorced, because there seemed to be no other option. We told him how appreciative we felt that he had never been judgmental toward either of us. He was my confidant, and confidant to my husband and children. Jorge always had an answer for every conflict and difficulty, not only for people in his family, but also for the "*familia politica*" [in-laws].[221]

Some people asked me why I was so determined to reach out to others when I needed help myself. I explained that touching the hearts of large crowds was momentarily uplifting; however, helping two people whom I dearly loved was more fulfilling.

That Thanksgiving, Gretchen and I flew to Tucson to attend a blessing ceremony for Clara, our *Clarita*. It was held around the fountain in the home of Kyria and her husband, Terry Pollock. Greta came in from New York, joined by her German beau. Tía Greta, who was inspired to dance with baby Clarita all over her new home, had been, I believe, "touched by the heavenly one."

Tía Greta holding baby Clarita on the day of her blessing— Kyria, Terry, and Jorge in the background

After spending Thanksgiving and Christmas in Tucson and Austin, I returned to Mexico City hoping to get the stem cell transplant. However, the surgeon informed me the surgery would not be possible at this time. Later my doctor suggested he could instead implant electrodes into my brain.

In June 2001, my nieces Ida, Silvia, and Martha accompanied me when I had my brain operation, which was far less painful than I had imagined. The surgery was performed at the prestigious Angeles del Pedregal Hospital. Ida and Martha later reported:

> At night he would want to stand up, and we kept trying to help him. He would say, "I can do it. I can do it myself. I want you to sleep, and if I need you I will let you know, but I can do it." As for the treatment, the technological experts kept trying to adjust the electrodes. And when they did, he thought for a time that he was better.[222]

Jorge with his nieces Ida (left) and Martha (right), March 1999

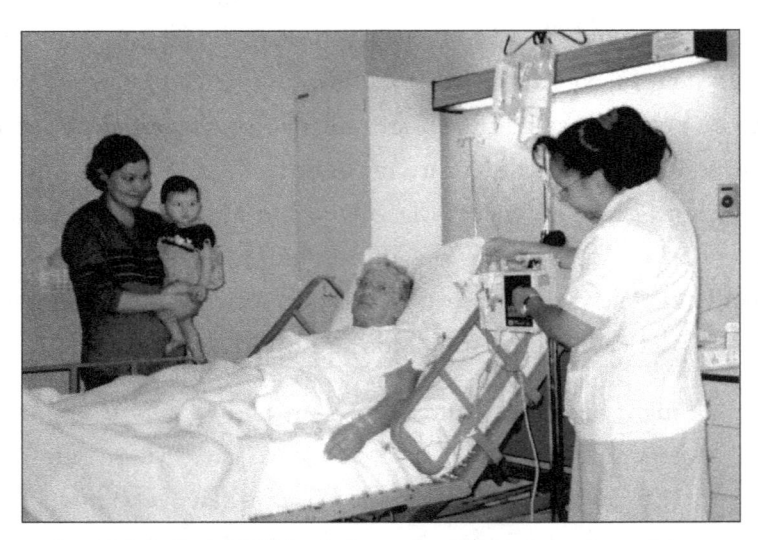

Jorge's niece Silvia Aduna holding her daughter, Sofia, in the hospital in Mexico City

Despite the operation, I failed to improve. One telling experience made Gretchen and me wonder if I was regressing. We had gone to Tucson for Thanksgiving in 2001, bringing with us a life-sized baby doll for Clara, partly to prepare her for the upcoming birth of her brother, Alexander Thomas. I tried and tried to open the present for her, but it was too much for me. Were the electrodes working at all?

Not only was the Parkinson's debilitating, the excruciating abdominal pain continued relentlessly. Early in 2003, Gretchen and I visited two surgeons in Houston asking them to remove the mesh from the my hernia operation. We hoped this would alleviate the problem. They both said this would not be possible.

In mid-April of that year, we went again to Houston for an overall examination of my brain, beginning with an MRI. Because of lifelong claustrophobia, the process was particularly frightening for me. During the MRI, the connection between the electrodes in my brain and the sensor holding the battery pack in my chest broke. Without further checking, the Houston doctors scheduled an operation to replace the battery pack and the connection. What the doctors discovered was worse than what we feared—the electrodes within my brain had been put in the wrong place and were not helping me at all.

Needless to say, we returned to Austin discouraged. The well-known surgeon in Mexico City had let me down—so had the medical team in Houston. Once home, I stayed in a darkened room and slept on the floor for several months, the hard surface being the most comfortable.

I felt so much despair that I even wrote a note that I had planned to give to Gretchen but never dared show her. I listed all the problems I was having: Parkinson's, agonizing abdominal pain, and a digestive problem that caused me to lose over fifty pounds in ten months. Moreover, I had a feeling of horrendous isolation in a world that at one time was familiar and friendly. I felt I had the right to go.[223]

While God seemed absent at times, my faith remained. Even if I died, I knew I would continue to live in God's love. Days and weeks would pass where I had absolutely nothing to give. I could see the suffering deepen in Gretchen's eyes and mirrored in the faces of our friends, who did their best to support me, but I could not respond.

Occasionally grace would intervene and a small gesture would rise, although I was as good as dead. I remember one afternoon when I was lying there, my eyes covered with a washcloth. As Gretchen left the room, she said: "*Ojitos*" (little eyes), a word we used with Clarita to mean blink. I made a small blinking motion with my hand. This sign of life thrilled her. That tiny action offered her a crumb of hope.[224]

Jorge and Gretchen

Later that summer, I opened my eyes for a moment and saw her standing there. I could imagine how lifeless I looked, lying pale, still sleeping on the floor. I whispered, "I want to write a letter thanking you for all you are doing." Much later, she told me that in hearing these words she knew I would live.[225]

During this time, I continued to measure my worthiness by how much "good" I was doing in the world. When I told Greta how useless I felt, she assured me I was even more life-giving to her and others close by, now that I was openly vulnerable and more available.

One day, Gretchen and I made our way down to the pool. It is set into the ground a level below the house. We designed it to look as though it belonged there. As we made our way slowly down the stairs, I was having trouble walking and said, "My legs are so stiff." Then Gretchen stepped ahead of me, beckoning me on. We made our way to the shallow end. I entered the water and she looked intently at me. I could read her love for me in her smiling eyes.

"Dance with me," I said. And we danced, drawing circles in the water with our arms, making music with the movement of our bodies. We didn't speak but danced slowly, like children, against the water's gentle resistance. Then, out of the silence, I said, "My body may be disabled but I can still love you."[226]

Close friends and family were justifiably concerned that I was losing my will to live. Gretchen invited Greta, Dan Weisser, her fiancé, her cousin Standish Meacham, Judith Liro, Lydia Huerta, and Mary Teague to pray for me. They all gathered around our dining room table one Saturday in late August. I listened as they read aloud parts of sermons I had given at El Buen Pastor. Afterward, they laid their hands on me and prayed fervently that I might be healed.

**Parishioners from El Buen Pastor Church
who came to pray with Jorge**

A few days later, our dear friend Chris Hines phoned. He was the chaplain at Christopher House, a "homelike" hospice facility in Austin. He suggested I come stay there. They offered me a room with windows looking out to a garden filled with colorful flowers. My doctor, Leigh Fredholm, a lovely, capable woman, gave me medications that eased my pain.

In mid-September, I told her I was like the paralytic in the Bible lifted by four friends through a hole they carved into the roof of a house where Jesus was healing people. As the pain meds eased my suffering, I began to see the light. Since Gretchen would be attending Greta's wedding in San Miguel de Allende, Mexico, that October, Dr. Fredholm and Chris allowed me to remain at Christopher House until her return. Because I could not attend the wedding, I sent this toast for Gretchen to read at their rehearsal dinner:

> I promised I would be present at your wedding. I am true to my word. My presence there is far more than physical.

It is rather a spiritual reality which knows no bounds. So this night, before your wedding, I raise a toast to Greta and Dan: "For me and everyone who loves you, you are the salt of the earth and the light of the world."[227]

Gretchen making a toast at Greta and Dan's wedding, October 11, 2003

After my surprising weeks of healing at Christopher House, I went home feeling more peaceful and hopeful than I had in a long time. Dr. Fredholm had partially redeemed the medical profession in my eyes. While my pain had not disappeared, it was more bearable. After feeling sure I was going to die, I revived. Amazingly to others, and most of all to me, I began to fall in love with life again.

Soon after I returned from Christopher House, an event occurred that confirmed my worthiness and boosted my spirits. Oscar Page, the president of Austin College, came to my home to give me the Austin College Distinguished Alumnus Award recognizing me for my decades of active service. That afternoon marked a transition for me. Afterward I began living a quieter life.

Later that same week, Cachuy and her daughters, Martha and Silvia, came up from Mexico. Having them in our home together with Greta and Dan, who were living nearby, was a great boost to my spirits. Their visits, the Austin College award, Dr. Fredholm's medical attention, our friends, and prayers—all helped bring me back to life. That December, I exclaimed to Gretchen, "My switch has gone on! I no longer feel depressed."[228]

During this period, Wynette Barton, a Jungian therapist, came to work with me every week. She accompanied me as I began to travel the uncharted waters of my unconscious during this new phase of my life. She encouraged me to pay close attention to my dreams, and helped me decipher their meaning. Through my dreams, she said, I could befriend my own unconscious.

I remember one dream where I was in a town in the northern part of Mexico, similar to Delicias, where I grew up. Much like me, perched between life and death, the town was located on the edge of a canyon. The occasion in the dream was the Annual Feast of Expectation, which was so appropriate for me as I was expecting and hoping to get well. There was a celebratory spirit—dancing and singing in Aramaic, the language of Jesus.

The whole town was full of people who were awaiting a messiah. The people said he would emerge one morning chanting while moving up from the river to the town. To be a part of their particular religious sect, one had to be hardworking, as I had been my whole life. The community invited me to speak. When I asked what I should say, the patriarch said I would know. I realized it was not the way I spoke but what I said that would indicate if I was to be the chosen one. When I started, there was an enormous commotion—geysers erupting, the river canyon breaking up. The people then cried out, "That's the proof, that is the proof, he is a messiah." When I noticed the danger, I called out to the people to leave before the river swallowed them.

The patriarch then took me and others away in his helicopter. The whole town, including the people who believed so strongly in hard work, were swallowed up by the river and were gone. However, the people did not think that was sad.[229]

The community's declaration that I was to be a messiah—a wild and preposterous idea—may have come from the fact that I had spoken so often of the Messiah in relation to his suffering. Being chosen as a messiah was not a sign of my superiority, but more an indication that God, who had been afar, was coming closer and seeking ways to comfort me. This declaration also served as a counterbalance to my own feelings of unworthiness and despair. The community's desire to have me as their leader confirmed I could still be useful. Their emphasis on what I said, rather than how I said it, showed the importance of being authentic, rather than focusing on my appearance. To me, it meant trusting in God and not worrying about my own success or failure.

Most of all, my dream signaled I was entering a new phase wherein I would neither be expected, nor expect, to prove myself by deeds. The town and the sect of people whose worth was based on hard work were washed away, just as that part of me needed to die. As Greta had suggested, now I hoped to find meaning in simply being a quiet and loving presence, allowing God's grace to flow through me.

During this new phase, Wynette and I spoke, from time to time, about my death, which no longer frightened me. She helped me to be grateful for the ways Gretchen and I had openly confronted our struggles. Like Cynthia Bourgeault, the author of *Love Is Stronger than Death*, Wynette believed that because we had struggled openly with our shadow sides together, we would have a greater possibility of a union beyond this life.[230] Realizing this helped me to be more accepting of my own death.

How terrible it would have been to have missed these last years. Though my pain had not disappeared, the experience of finding my inner spirit was truly a miracle, when just a few months before I had not even wanted to continue living.

A special source of joy was the arrival of new babies in our family. A few months after my revival at Christopher House, Kyria came for a visit together with Clarita and her younger brother, Xander. Before meals, we used to congregate in my bedroom. Though Xander was not quite two years old, he was very attentive to me. While everyone else was busy talking, Xander took me by the hand, time after time, and led me to the bathroom.

Xander hugging Jorge

A few years later, Greta also had her first child, Maxwell. When they came to Austin, I used to ask Max if he had a message from God. Many afternoons, I invited him to nap with me, believing that by lying close to him I was becoming closer to God. Like his cousins, Max himself was the message—so caring for others from the time he was born.

Jorge taking a walk with Maxwell and Greta

In 2007, Gretchen flew to Dubai to welcome Maxwell's sister, Leela. From the time of her birth, Leela had been stricken with painful eczema. So during her first and only summer with me, she cried a lot. She seemed to love my voice, and I liked carrying and singing to her. Greta said I was the only one who could calm her.

Judith holding baby Leela, with Jorge and Gretchen, December 2007

Greta, Maxwell, and Gretchen were amazed to see me carrying Leela back and forth in the yard for long periods of time. Being with Leela and the other little ones comforted and energized me. In some mysterious way, they strengthened my faith. Perhaps it was because they themselves had so recently come from God's realm, where I would soon be going.

Afterword

"¡Se siente, se siente que Jorge está presente!"
(It Feels, It Feels Like Jorge Is Here!)

by Gretchen Lara-Shartle

Late in the afternoon, on Wednesday, June 18, 2008, Jorge was walking with a friend. He fell on the trail just above our home and slipped immediately into unconsciousness. Greta and her two children had just arrived that afternoon from Dubai to spend the summer. Together with two friends, she and I followed the ambulance to the Brackenridge Hospital Emergency Room. We learned right away that Jorge had broken his neck in three places. Because he was unconscious, the hospital placed him on a breathing machine. They also planned to ice him down to prevent further deterioration of his brain.

The next morning, Greta, our niece Ida, Greta's children, along with beloved friends Judith Liro and Eileen Lundy, all went to the hospital together. Of course, we hoped for a miracle—to find Jorge conscious. He was not. Amidst our tears we cried out, "*¡Se siente, se siente que Jorge está presente!*" (It feels, it feels like Jorge is here!). Jorge had shouted this declaration with hundreds of Salvadorans at Monseñor Romero's funeral. We had also shouted this phrase together in Nicaragua when we remembered the scores of innocents who had been murdered. As we called out those words, that Thursday morning in Jorge's intensive care room, Jorge raised his eyebrows and my heart leapt.

By June 20, our Austin friends, Jorge Luis and the family from Mexico City, even Dan from Dubai had begun to arrive at the hospital. We could not help breaking the rule to have no more than three people in the room at once. We cried, prayed, and sang, "*Ubi Caritas et amor, Deus ibi est*" (Wherever compassion and love are, God is always present).

AFTERWORD

Jorge Luis and Jorge in 2007

Shortly before Jorge died on June 22, over twenty people held hands and stood in a circle around his bed. I sat close beside him, holding his right hand very tightly in my own, as I said with all my heart over and over, "You will be a part of me and I will be a part of you forever and ever."

Jorge died around two o'clock that afternoon. Greta and I left Brackenridge Hospital together. More than anything, I told her how I would miss his fearlessness and adventurous spirit. How exciting it had been to chase him on my bike in France and in Austin, when we rode to El Buen Pastor. On those rides, as in every part of our lives, we seldom stuck to the usual trails.

Gretchen and Jorge outside El Buen Pastor, November 20, 2000

The word *destiny* had no personal meaning for me until after Jorge died. Then I saw how incredible it was that we met and soon after joined our lives and our spirits so completely. We were born in different countries and were from two contrasting cultures. While Jorge spent part of his teen years in a Mexico City tenement, I spent my youth in a large home on fifty acres of pine trees.

That first summer after his death was the hardest for me. At grace, before meals at home, when our family sang "*Ubi Caritas*," I felt bereft and wondered where God was. All my inner pathways seemed to be blocked by thick cement barricades. That's when I received a Rumi poem from a Muslim friend that helped me feel freer:

AFTERWORD

"The Wonderful Results of Taming"
A lovesick nightingale among owls
caught the scent of roses
and flew to the rose garden.[231]

I imagined myself moving beyond the cement barricades by following the scent of roses. More than anything, I wanted an actual sign showing Jorge was near. "Where are you?" I silently asked. "How can I walk this thin line between my presence here and yours on the other side? Will I ever see you again?"

In August, Greta and the children would be leaving for Dubai. I dreaded Greta's departure. That is when the most remarkable thing happened. We began to see tiny, fragrant white flowers blooming in trees around the house, even down by the garden. We had never seen them before. At first, I wondered where they had come from; then we realized these Sweet Autumn Clematis had come from Jorge.

Sweet Autumn Clematis now blooms all around our home.

Being with Jorge for twenty-two years was thrilling, but living alone with him for those last five years was wonderful too. We loved our times alone; even spending Christmas Day with no one but Jorge was special. Our walks together, as I breathlessly read the Bible aloud, were a joy. If I stopped reading, even for a moment, he'd say, "Keep on!"

Our loving base often became a springboard to reach out to others nearby and faraway. It was absolutely glorious to me that Jorge and I had the same passions: housing for the poor, struggles of Salvadoran and Nicaraguan people in the 1980s, and standing up for Mexican and Central American immigrants.

Over and over, people identified me as his "caregiver." They failed to understand that he was my caregiver—my pastor—to the end. Perhaps it was because he himself had suffered so greatly that he understood when I and others were challenged. So often, he was my sanctuary. When I was faced with a seemingly unsolvable difficulty, Jorge found a creative solution. He calmed me like no one else ever had. He listened, understood, and had compassion. Even when his mysterious pain was so intense that he had to take morphine, he remained my spiritual rock. He spoke glowingly of my cheerfulness and courageous determination. What he may not have realized is that even during those last years, when he was in excruciating pain and anesthetized by morphine, my "*Sí se puede*" spirit came from him.

Jorge had become an integral part of my family. Jorge and Greta were true friends and often traveled together. She seldom made a big decision without asking for his advice and blessing. Kyria, too, sought Jorge's counsel. In fact, when she and Terry married, they invited Jorge to wed them. He endeared himself to Terry by including his Jewish traditions in the ceremony. He found a way to

AFTERWORD

make a *chuppah*, a traditional arched Jewish wedding tent. Even my dad, who was so cautious when he first met Jorge, came to love him.

Jorge officiating at Terry and Kyria's wedding in Tucson— Greta (right) as maid of honor, March 4, 2000

Among my friends, one of his favorites was our beloved friend and pastor Judith Liro. When she preached at his memorial held at El Buen Pastor, she began by calling out to him:

> Jorge! Jorge! How we wish you could preach at your own funeral today. You would passionately call us to justice. You would touch our hearts and bring tears to our eyes. You would bring smiles and laughter to comfort our sadness. You would transform us with a story. We already miss you, Jorge! We miss you so much!

> When I was driving to the Emergency Room, one week ago tonight, I sensed that Jorge would be fine no matter what. At that point, I knew he had been without oxygen for at least ten minutes, so I expected his death

and trusted his eventual well-being in the arms of God. Driving toward Brackenridge, I felt peaceful about Jorge, but my heart cried out for dear beloved Gretchen, and for the web of family and friends whose lives have been sustained by Jorge's love and being. We are the ones who will be challenged to transform the emptiness of great loss into a sense of ongoing presence. My life has been so blessed by his wisdom and wit, by his elegant mind, and his generous heart. I am one of those who is left bereft.

In the last few days as I opened my heart to what could be said on this occasion, I realized that Jorge has preached a sermon for tonight. It is more than quotations from sermons he's given in the past, more than any theological writings. It is a sermon that includes and yet is more than words, gestures, and presence in the pulpit. Jorge! Tonight and tomorrow and in the days to come we'll cherish the sermon you preached us with your life.

In 1 Corinthians 6:19 we read, "You must know that your body is a temple of the Holy Spirit, who is within you—the Spirit you have received from God." For Jorge, each person's body was the temple of the Holy Spirit. Jorge could sense and respond to the true worth, the high value, of each one individually. His understanding that each body was a lion of courage and something precious to the earth, that each person was "a temple of the Holy Spirit," was the basis for his passionate cry for justice. Since all persons are of infinite worth, then all should share in the blessings of life. All should have food, shelter, opportunities for health, for friendship and community.

AFTERWORD

At this point when all is still fresh and raw, I am aware that Jorge's life is holy for me. This holiness has nothing to do with sinlessness; Jorge did make a mess of things at times, as many, if not most, of us have. For me the word "holy" is connected not with purity but with the word "whole," with the fullness of living as an authentic human being. Jorge's life was whole. He experienced both the mountain top of triumph and the pit of despair. He achieved great prominence as a theologian, teacher, and activist. He also knew the depths of failure. He continued to grow throughout his life, to become a wonderful family man as well as a larger-than-life prophet. He experienced not only health and energy as a youthful, tireless reformer but also the frailty and indignity of illness and the delight of being "Lito," beloved grandfather. Although he could be the first to reach out to someone bent over with personal failure, at times Jorge struggled to realize he was among the forgiven. The physical diminishment, which grieved and challenged him so, could never extinguish that radiance within, even though at times he lost touch with it himself. Jorge fought for life to the end in body, mind, and spirit, and then Sister Death walked him across the chasm into the arms of God.

Jorge, you were *the bridegroom, taking the world into your arms* and including us in your embrace! As we listen to the sermon of your life, inspire us, Jorge, to make of ourselves something particular and real. *Dance in our hearts as we marry amazement and take the world into our arms in our own way.*[232] Show us the way to kindness and to the welcoming presence. You saw Jesus in us and we saw Jesus in you. Go in peace, beloved teacher and friend. We love you. Amen.[233]

Kyria sprinkling dirt in Jorge's grave; Gretchen is behind Judith Liro, who presided over his funeral in Austin, June 26, 2008

Clara's drawing of her dream of playing hopscotch in heaven with Jorge, November 2008

Acknowledgments

Creating *Dare to Adventure, Las Bienaventuranzas: The Life of Jorge Lara-Braud* has been a team effort. Fortuitously, Joella Werlin, my high school friend, who specializes in writing family histories, came for a visit in 2007. She was so inspired when she met Jorge that she voluntarily returned from Oregon and did a series of interviews with him. Those materials, called "Mi Jornada," formed the basis of the early chapters. Without her surprising gift, this book may not have been possible.

A few months after Jorge died in 2008, our beloved friend Walter Wink, a biblical scholar known for his nonviolent political activism, tried to publish *Dare to Adventure: Bienaventuranza* (the original title). At that time, it was a compilation of Joella's interviews and Jorge's sermons and speeches. When his efforts did not work out, Walter and his wife, June, encouraged me to go forth and continue writing Jorge's story.

Soon after, I began to weave the threads of Jorge's life story into a more complete narrative. His sister, María de Jesús Lara de Espino (Cachuy), helped to fill in the family picture, as did his son, Jorge Luis Lara Marroquín, and his nieces Silvia Espino Aduna and Ida Garcia de Espino. Standish Meacham, my cousin-in-law, edited the earliest version. I am grateful to each person for their participation.

Joella Werlin and Jorge working outside on "Mi Jornada," at Gretchen and Jorge's home, April 2005

Pastor and initiator of the Sanctuary Movement in the United States, John Fife graciously wrote the foreword for the book. José Luis Velazco Medina, pastor and former Secretary of the General Assembly of the National Presbyterian Church in Mexico, and a close friend of Jorge's, generously consulted with me in explaining the meaning of "Las Bienaventuranzas" from a Latino perspective.

Lois Silverstein, a professional editor, collaborated closely with me. Her insights were instrumental in the early development of this book. My friends and other collaborators—Pastor Judith Liro, JoLynn Free, Mary Teague, Tammy Ramirez, Shannon Armstrong, Pastor Tim Lanham, former Catholic priest Ed

ACKNOWLEDGMENTS

Lundy, Jim Crosby, Jan Williams, and Terry Pollock—have all been wonderfully supportive and given tirelessly of their editorial expertise. Daphne Levey and Jane Walton have added spirited ideas for titles. From the beginning, Kristy Sorenson, at the Austin Presbyterian Theological Seminary library, assisted in fact checking and research, and Rana Perucci helped throughout the entire process. Bob Fullilove has played an essential role in editing, formatting, and completing the manuscript.

I am ever so grateful to Linda Amala Puckett for working with me in finding a publisher and seeking ways to send Jorge's message forth.

Leticia Gutierrez has been supportive, cooking delicious meals and encouraging me during every phase of this book's creation. Greta Weisser has enthusiastically supported me from the beginning of this project. And Kyria Sabin has worked diligently with me in designing the cover.

I feel deeply thankful to each one of you who joined me in this adventure. *Dare to Adventure, Las Bienaventuranzas: The Life of Jorge Lara-Braud* is our book, not mine alone! Muchas gracias to each one of you.

Appendix A

1492–1992: Can We Believe in God after This?
—A lecture presented by Jorge Lara-Braud at the Austin Presbyterian Theological Seminary, Columbus Day, 1992

Preliminary note: This essay attempts to be a theological reflection on the legacy of Columbus's arrival five hundred years ago. It focuses primarily on the Spanish colonization of the first decades, as it was possibly what most influenced the future of the Americas.

I. Columbus: The Christ-Bearer

At dawn on August 3, 1492, Columbus left the port of Palos, Spain, in command of three vessels: *la Santa María, la Pinta,* and *la Niña.* After eight years of entreaties, he had persuaded the most

Catholic sovereigns of Spain, Isabella and Ferdinand, to sponsor his visionary project of reaching the Indies on a voyage from east to west. It was a venture for which there was no precedent. Many European influentials, especially seasoned navigators, predicted total failure. The skepticism had as much to do with doubtful cartographic calculations as with the problematic personality of the leader. Columbus was supremely sure of himself, often resorting to esoteric knowledge gleaned from the Bible and mystical experiences to buttress his certainty and to silence his critics.[1]

Reading the record of the many actors and factors that led to the launching of Columbus's adventure, one is impressed by an omnipresent religiousness, replete with references to the perceived will of God. It can be safely assumed that without some sense of divine sanction, a project so formidably questionable might not have been attempted.

The moment could not have been more religious. 1492 marks the year of the final Christian victory over the Moorish "infidel" after eight centuries of ceaseless struggle. It marks also the expulsion of the Jews from Spain, putting an end to their commanding presence in Spanish life after about half a millennium. The Moors had surrendered at Granada only two months before. The deadline for the departure of the Jews was set for August 2 at midnight. Columbus left a few hours later. As a matter of fact, he tried to leave earlier, but the Spanish ports had been tied up for months,

---

[1] Among the many biographies of Columbus in English, the best are probably these three: Hans Koning, *Columbus: His Enterprise* (New York: Monthly Review Press, 1976); Samuel Eliot Morison, *Admiral of the Ocean Sea* (Boston: Little, Brown, 1942), 2 vols.; and Paolo Taviani, *Christopher Columbus: The Grand Design* (London: Orbis Books, 1985). Koning's is quite critical, Morison's frankly laudatory, and Taviani's soberly calibrated.

while some 200,000 of the ancient People of God desperately tried to beat the deadline.[2]

In lavish religious ceremonies and in numberless theological treatises, vindication over Jews and Muslims was celebrated as a direct intervention of God. God had brought Spain to this moment of greatness in preparation for larger conquests still, for the expansion of Christianity, and for the greater glory of God. No wonder an experienced navigator who saw himself as chosen by God to open Asia to the gospel of Jesus Christ could win over the most Catholic monarchs to his cause. Was not his name Cristófero (Christ-bearer) and Colón (colonizer)? This was manifest destiny indeed.[3]

There were, of course, motivations other than religious ones. The crown stood to gain untold wealth from the dominion of vast lands. Columbus, in turn, not only assured himself of titles of great honor, but also of munificent perquisites. He was knighted, appointed Grand Admiral and Viceroy (titles to remain in his family forever), and guaranteed 10 percent of any transactions within his admiralty. Even these benefits were seen within the plan of God. In a letter to Queen Isabella following his first trip, Columbus expressed the hope that she might voluntarily devote as much as possible of the wealth from the new domains to finance the huge military effort it would take to rescue Jerusalem from

---

2 Hunter Davies, *In Search of Columbus* (London: Sinclair Stevenson, 1991), 85.

3 This is how Columbus understands his appointment in a letter to the Catholic sovereigns: "Your Highnesses, as good Christians and Catholic princes, devout and propagators of the Christian faith, as well as enemies of the sect of Mahomet and of all idolatries and heresies, conceived the plan of sending me, Christopher Columbus, to this country of the Indies, there to see the princes, the people, the territory, their dispositions and all things else, and the way in which one might proceed to convert these regions to our holy faith." Quoted in H. McKennie, *Goodpasture, Cross and Sword* (Maryknoll, N.Y.: Orbis Books, 1989), 7.

the infidels, thereby bringing the gains of discovery under the plan and blessing of God.[4]

At dawn, on October 12, 1492, Columbus set foot on an island of the New World. It was the idyllically beautiful Guanahani, one of the Bahama islands. The Admiral of the Sea proceeded immediately to rename it San Salvador, in honor of Jesus Christ, the Savior of the world. Carrying the royal banner, and planting a cross, he took possession of the island in the name of Ferdinand and Isabella, God's stewards of all the new lands. Of course, he was sure he had landed at the edge of the Orient, a conviction he strengthened as he wandered among more lovely islands, giving them new Spanish names to honor saints and the Catholic monarchs.

Irrespective of any doubt we might have about the motives or consequences of Columbus's arrival in the New World, it was an awesome accomplishment, if we take into account how inadequate were the technology, the vessels, the provisions, and especially the maps. It is understandable why so many have looked upon it as an intervention of God, or at least as a true watershed in the history of humanity. This is no doubt what in 1942 Samuel Eliot Morison, Columbus's most influential modern biographer, was reaching for in language which today sounds impossibly sexist:

> Never again may mortal men hope to recapture the amazement, the wonder, the delight, of those October days in 1492 when the New World gracefully yielded her virginity to the conquering Castilians.[5]

---

[4] Bartolomé de Las Casas cites the letter in his *Historia de Las Indias*, ed. Agustín Millares Carlo, with an introduction by Lewis Hanke (Mexico City: Fondo de Cultura Económica, 1951), 1:30.

[5] Morison, *Admiral of the Ocean Sea*, 45.

APPENDIX A

A leading Spanish church historian, Francisco López de Gómara, writing sixty years after Columbus's arrival, referred to it as "the greatest event since the creation of the world, excluding the incarnation and the death of him who created it." And Adam Smith, the father of capitalism, was moved to say: "The discovery of America and that of the passage to the East Indies by the Cape of Good Hope, are the greatest and most important events recorded in the history of humankind."[6]

But we cannot stay too long in the realm of admiration. The feat, surrounded as it was with so much association with God, very quickly led to justify actions that were to become inhuman practices for a great deal of subsequent colonial history. A harbinger of things to come took place on the very day of Columbus's arrival. Not finding gold, he took by force six slaves from Guanahani, to bring them to the Catholic monarchs on his return as some kind of trophy.[7]

There is irony here. Columbus's enterprise was justified chiefly on religious grounds, namely, to bring pagans to the knowledge of the Christian God. Curiously, out of 90 men making the first voyage, there was no member of the clergy. That is to say that no one was charged with the responsibility to preach the gospel or to baptize. God's design, instead, was left to the pious Admiral, whose first significant dealing with the natives was not to bring them the good news of Jesus Christ, but to reduce six of them to slavery. Tragically, the record shows that this was to be the sense of priorities for the system of theocratic domination that began in

---

[6] National Council for the Social Studies, "The Columbian Quincentenary: An Educational Opportunity," *History Teacher* 25, no. 2 (February 1992): 142–52.

[7] John Cummins, *The Voyage of Christopher Columbus: Columbus' Own Journal of Discovery, Newly Restored and Translated* (London: Weidenfeld and Nicolson, 1991), 94. The journal entry is dated October 11. It actually corresponds to the next day, his first day in the New World.

the New World on October 12, 1492, and that continues to this day, no longer, perhaps, in the name of the Christian God, but in the name of other divinities.

The lands which Columbus "discovered" on his first trip were three Bahamian islands, plus Cuba and Hispaniola (the large island occupied today by Haiti and the Dominican Republic). Upon his return, he described them as paradises populated by childlike natives. About these natives, he writes in his diary on the very day of his arrival in the New World: "They must be good servants, and intelligent, for I can see that they quickly repeat everything said to them. I believe they would readily become Christians; it appeared to me that they have no religion."[8] And in a letter he wrote to the Catholic monarchs on his return from that first voyage, he states: "Slaves can be shipped, as many as shall be ordered, who will be idolaters."[9]

Within two months of Columbus's return, Pope Alexander VI, as vicar of Christ and successor to Saint Peter, signed a series of four bulls donating to the Spanish sovereigns the newly discovered lands and any others yet to be discovered by subjects of the Spanish crown. Together they were to legitimize for the next three hundred years the entire enterprise of the Spanish conquest and colonization of Latin America. The first was issued May 3, 1493; the fourth and last, September 26 of the same year. Statements like these signal what to the pope was the purpose of the new and later discoveries:

> that the Catholic faith and the Christian religion may be propagated and extended everywhere to secure the salvation of souls, the subjection of barbarous nations,

---

[8] Ibid.
[9] Davies, *In Search of Columbus*, 140.

and to bring them into our faith . . . that Christ's empire may be increased . . . that those dwellers and nations may come under the subjection and the service of our Redeemer Lord.[10]

The stage was set for deliberate conquest in the name of evangelization, all with God's blessing, and Columbus was more than ready again to do honor to his name as the Christ-bearer. On September 25, 1493, he started on his second trip, which was to last almost three years. This time the fleet numbered seventeen ships carrying more than 1,200 men, of whom only two were priests. This trip proved to be crucial. As Hans Koning, the Dutch American historian and novelist, has said of it:

> The pattern was set for time to come. The pretense was ended; the idyll over. The Indians who had been praised for their generosity and innocence, were now called savages. The talk was of slavery and gold, rather than brotherhood or conversion.[11]

II. If Not Gold, Then Slaves

A great deal of the expectation and optimism surrounding this second trip had to do with the certainty that this time, with more men, and better technology and weapons, vast amounts of gold

---

[10] The first three papal bulls are *Inter caetera* and *Eximiae devotionis* (dated May 3, 1493) and *Inter caetera* (2nd one dated May 4). The fourth papal bull is *Dudum siquidem* on September 26, 1493. Collectively they make up the Bulls of Donation. Bartolomé de Las Casas, *Tratados de Fray Bartolomé de Las Casas*, trans. Juan Pérez de Tudela Bueso, Agustín Millares Carlo, and Rafael Moreno (Mexico City: Fondo de Cultura Económica, 1997), 2:1277–82. (Here, as elsewhere, where a work cited bears a title in Spanish, the English text translation is Jorge's.)

[11] John Yewell and Chris Dodge, "The Second Voyage," in *Confronting Columbus: An Anthology* (Jefferson, N.C.: McFarland & Company, 1992), 48.

would be found and secured in the new lands. But, as time went by, disappointment began to set in. What little gold the Spaniards found in Hispaniola, Cuba, Puerto Rico, and the present West Indies was worn as ornaments by the Indians, and here and there used in minimal amounts to decorate their sacred places. In sum, no deposits of gold of any importance were found anywhere on this journey. The consequences were fatal for the Indians. Here again I turn to Koning for a summary description:

> There were no gold fields, and thus, once the Indians had handed in whatever they still had in gold ornaments, their only hope was to work all day in the streams, washing out gold dust from the pebbles. It was an impossible task, but those Indians who tried to flee into the mountains were systematically hunted down with dogs and killed, to set an example for the others to keep on trying.
>
> Thus it was at this time that the mass suicides began: the Arawaks killed themselves with casaba poison.

Koning also reminds us that during those two years of the administration of Columbus and his brothers, Diego and Bartolomé, an estimated one-half of the entire population of Hispaniola was killed or killed themselves. The estimates run from 125,000 to 500,000.[12]

Even Samuel Eliot Morison, who perhaps more than any other biographer has idealized the memory of Columbus, admits: "The cruel policy initiated by Columbus and pursued by his successors resulted in complete genocide."[13]

---

12 Koning, *Columbus*, 53–54.
13 Samuel Eliot Morison, *Christopher Columbus: Mariner* (New York: New American Library, 1942), 99.

We are right when we associate gold and the conquest of Latin America. But that had to wait for the Spanish invasion of Mexico by Cortés in 1519 and of Peru by Pizarro in 1530. In the meantime, from the time of Columbus's second voyage, Indian slavery made up for the absence of gold. Thus, in February 1495, Columbus rounded up some 1,500 Arawaks, including women and children, and because the ships available could not carry so many, he personally chose the 500 best specimens to be sold in Spain.[14] The crown, in turn, expecting that the slave trade might prove immensely profitable, issued the first laws regulating it as early as 1501, three years before Columbus would complete his fourth and final voyage.[15] Somehow the crown's canon lawyers managed to reconcile evangelization and the selling and buying of human beings.

Of course, the moment human beings are bought and sold, a statement has been made that life is relative, as if it were property or merchandise—even if the marginal condition of the victims may hide the magnitude of the violation. In order to perpetrate something like this in a society ruled by law, and particularly in a society where law is derived in some way from the law of God, requires the very best talent to make it appear that there is no fracture in the convictions shared by rulers and subjects. Here the theologians and other custodians of ultimate truths make the difference, both by what they say and by what they do not say. This is what happened in Spain beginning with Columbus, and what has happened to this day in every country that needs to justify its domination of others, whether as actual slaves or as pawns of economic policy.

---

14 Koning, *Columbus*, 85.
15 Ibid.

One has to say more. Even after slavery is abrogated by law, a long history of legitimized abuse has formed attitudes and habits that are enormously difficult to break. The beneficiaries have internalized a sense of their own superiority—a superiority related to protected status, influential connections, preferential treatment by the law, favored physical characteristics, aesthetic enjoyments, credentialed education, the daily exercise of real and symbolic power, and a sense of privileged relation to the ultimate.

There is, furthermore, a structural reason why these attitudes and habits are so hard to break. It has to do with the inertial power of the model of social organization that consolidates itself in the formative stages of a nation. What people of influence believe and enforce as normative in the beginning will continue to replicate itself in orthodoxies and patterns centuries thereafter. This is why we, as people of faith, do well to consider the legacy of what began 500 years ago in the name of God, and to be bold enough to ask whether, in the light of such a legacy, we can still believe in God. To put the question that way may seem extreme. But it is not. Not if we read the record from the perspective of those who paid the price and who are paying it still.

III. But the Search for Gold Is Still On

As profitable as slavery proved to be, gold continued to be the real enticement for consolidating the colonization of the New World. Columbus understood this. In a rambling narrative letter he wrote to the Catholic monarchs following his fourth and final trip, he included this doxology: "Oh most excellent gold! Who has gold has a treasure with which he gets what he wants, imposes his will on the world, and even helps souls to paradise."[16] The monarchs

---

16 Davies, *In Search of Columbus*, 264.

did not need the doxology. That was their conviction already. Everything they and their successors did in the New World fleshed it out.

Much of the exploratory activity launched at the beginning of the 16th century from the established footholds like Hispaniola and Cuba was in search of Indian slaves to replace the many who had died under forced labor or who had taken their own lives. In the search for gold, tantalizing prospects were found in Cuba, Puerto Rico, Central America, the North Atlantic coast of South America, and in Yucatán. Columbus's unfinished project of finding a waterway to the Orient was not abandoned. The culmination came with Magellan's 1519–22 circumnavigation of the globe. However, it was so commercially unprofitable that it led the Spanish to concentrate their colonizing efforts on the American continents.

They concentrated a great deal on the most decisive socioeconomic institution of colonization, the encomienda—literally, an entrustment. To create settlements capable of self-sufficiency and of generating tax revenues for the crown, but also to keep faith with the papal bulls of donation, which made the evangelization of the natives the chief purpose of colonization, colonists were entrusted with land and a generous quantity of Indians to perform all the necessary labor. In exchange for their labor, the Indians were housed, fed and evangelized. Was there ever a system of human exploitation more piously devised? Notice what the colonial authorities of the island of Hispaniola were to do to make it work, according to the royal decree of December 20, 1503, that legalized it. Notice also the pointed reference to gold:

> Hereafter, you are to compel and urge said Indians to mingle and converse with the Christians (the Spaniards)

of said Island and to work in their buildings, in gathering and extracting gold and other metals, in tilling the lands and raising food for the Christian neighbors and dwellers of said Island.... But the Indians are to do that as free persons, which they are, and not as servants.[17]

We can see how the legalization of the encomienda by the crown forced evangelization to rely on a system of inevitable slavery. The confusion of ends and means should not surprise us. Governments that see themselves as instruments of the highest inevitably destroy the very people they would save. What those governments require, if they are not to do even greater damage, is relentless critics from within who question the synonymity of interests between religion and the state, and who indeed can call the state to account also in the name of the highest. Of course, this is singularly the vocation of preachers and theologians who will not be co-opted. Fortunately for the Indians, such preachers and theologians began to arrive in the New World, at first in small numbers, as early as 1505. They were members of missionary orders, first Franciscans, and then, in quick succession, Dominicans, Mercedarians, Augustinians, and somewhat later, Jesuits. To such orders we owe not only a spirited defense of the Indians, but also the theological insistence that there must be a clear distinction between the god of the abusers and the God of the abused.

IV. By What Right?

By the time the Dominicans, led by Pedro de Córdoba, arrived in Hispaniola in 1510, the ravages of the encomienda system had begun to take an appalling toll. These Dominicans found astonishing

---

17 Gustavo Gutiérrez, *Dios o el oro de las Indias* (Lima: Instituto Bartolomé de Las Casas, 1989), 25–26.

how those who benefited from a legalized system of oppression could become so indifferent to the suffering they inflicted on others, while claiming to be led by high ethical and religious values. The friars did not wait long to make a public condemnation of that system. On the fourth Sunday of Advent of 1511 in the cathedral of Santo Domingo, speaking for all of them, Antonio Montesinos directed these words to a congregation made up of the governor, other influentials, and rank-and-file colonists:

> This voice (the voice of Christ) declares that you are in mortal sin, and live and die in it by reason of the cruelty and tyranny that you practice on these innocent people. Tell me, by what right and justification do you hold these Indians in such cruel and horrible servitude? By what authority do you wage such detestable wars on these people who lived in lands tranquil and peaceful, where you have consumed such an infinite number of them with unheard-of murders and desolations? How can you so oppress them and exhaust them, without feeding them or healing their diseases, when they fall ill from the excessive toil you put them under and from which they die, more truthfully, when you kill them to extract and come up with gold each day? And what care do you take that they receive religious instruction so they may know their God and creator, or that they may be baptized, hear Mass, or observe feast days and Sundays?
>
> Are they not human beings? Have they not rational souls? Are you not under the obligation to love them as you love yourselves? Have you no feelings? How can

you lie in such a deep and lethargic slumber? Be assured that in your present state you are no more capable of being saved than Moors or Turks, who do not have nor want faith in Jesus Christ.[18]

The audience was shocked and demanded an immediate retraction. The Dominicans closed ranks. The following Sunday, Montesinos repeated the charges, this time even more eloquently. Still, to no avail. No one seems to have been converted. But the lines had been drawn. For the next four centuries, the same voice was to be raised over and over again, at times clamorous, at times faint, until the present day, when it has been taken up massively by the Christian poor of the continent and their friends: priests, religious orders, theologians, ecumenical partners, and even bishops. That voice continues to demand that the distinction be made between the god of the abusers and the God of the abused.

We owe the account of Montesinos's sermon in the Santo Domingo cathedral to Bartolomé de Las Casas. Las Casas was to become the most celebrated defender of the Indians and the most reliable historian of their struggle for survival. But for a time he himself, as a priest and as a plantation owner, had profited from and legitimized the system of Indian oppression. His conversion to the cause of the abused had much to do with the courageous example of the Hispaniola Dominicans. In 1514, at the age of thirty, he gave up his properties in Cuba and joined the Dominicans in Santo Domingo. He could no longer plead ignorance.[19] It is supremely unfortunate that Las Casas advocated for a time replacing Indian with African slaves in the naive belief that their superior physical constitution might help them resist more successfully the

---

18 Las Casas, *Tratados*, 441–42.
19 Ibid., 93–95.

demands of forced labor and the threat of illness. It was not long before he acknowledged his error, from which he repented in agony of soul and spirit, adding to his repentance a tireless, spirited, and specific condemnation of African slavery.[20] What hounded Las Casas's conscience was that he had witnessed how, within eight years of the legalization of the encomienda system, 90 percent of the Indian population of Hispaniola had perished mainly from forced labor, and, as he was to write later, that "sweeping plague went to San Juan, Jamaica, Cuba and the continent, spreading destruction over the whole hemisphere."[21]

V. The Sweeping Plague

The sweeping plague Las Casas writes about would become the most massive genocide human history has ever known. Scholars agree somewhat conservatively that between 1492 and 1650, the Indian population of the continent dropped from about 54 million to less than 6 million, a net loss of 48 million, or 88 percent of the population.[22]

The causes of this incredible carnage are not all due to forced labor, although it is one of the principal ones. Other causes are malnutrition and suicide, but the most deadly one is the complex of contagious diseases the Europeans brought with them for which the native population had no immunity. The combination of exploitation and contagion turned into the "sweeping plague"

---

20 Ibid., 487–88. See his heartfelt, penitential, and testimonial reflections, especially in bk. 3, chap. 129.
21 Las Casas, *Historia de Las Indias*, 109–15.
22 See the most comprehensive review of these estimates in William M. Denevan, *The Native Population of the Americas in 1492* (Madison: University of Wisconsin Press, 1976), esp. xxix and 291. Taking into account the works of many other demographers, and placing himself roughly in between the maximum and minimum numbers, Professor Denevan himself estimates that the native population dropped from 53.9 million in 1492 to 5.6 million by 1650.

that made almost all the Indians of the New World die before their time. To put it starkly, it was death first of all, massive death, that these Europeans claiming the blessing God brought to the very ones they would save. And, of course, that deadly legacy is far from over. Yes, they did also bring Christianity, but at a price that called in question its saving promise and the God of that promise.

It took until the late 17th century for the Indian populations to begin to stabilize again and grow. But the European legacy of death was by no means over. It continues to this day. All it takes to prove it is to read current statistical reports on nutrition, health, housing, economic standing, and the life expectancy of the Indian, mestizo, and Afro-American peoples of the Americas, including the United States. Vast numbers continue to die before their time, and before they die, their life is a daily dying.

VI. Does the Christian God Also Love Pagans?

Bartolomé de Las Casas tried desperately to avoid this outcome by documenting the killing in the name of God that was going on in his time in the Caribbean islands, in Central America, in Mexico and Peru. He used his connections with influential government and church officials in Spain to publicize the abuses and to have laws enacted to protect the Indians. He made repeated trips across the Atlantic and gave up his bishopric in Chiapas to make the case in person. To his credit, the most enlightened laws regulating the treatment of the Indians were passed by three successive royal governments in his lifetime based on his powerful arguments. We also owe to him the basis for the most explicit defense of the Indians found in a papal pronouncement, Pope Paul III's bull Sublimis Deus of June 2, 1537, affirming that Indians, whether already

Christian or still outside the faith, "are not to be deprived of their liberty or the right to their property," and that, "should anything different be done, it is void, invalid, of no force, of no worth."[23]

Why, then, in spite of such laws did the carnage go on? Because humanitarian laws do not fare well when they interfere with the self-interest of those called to enforce them. Colonial authorities could always find exceptions, arguing it was to uphold the right of the crown to tax revenues, in part to finance the work of evangelization. It was this perverse logic that led Las Casas eventually to argue that it was preferable for an Indian to remain an infidel and live than to become a Christian and die.[24]

At best, then, the laws protecting the Indians may have slowed down the sweeping plague of death. What else could have helped? A major historical answer was the work of the missionary orders to which we have made reference. During the 16th, 17th, and 18th centuries, the Indians found a significant degree of safety in areas where the missionary orders functioned both as church emissaries and colonial officials. Unfortunately, that kind of safety was tragically undermined by the missionaries themselves. They dealt a shattering blow to the very heart of Indian identity: one's relationship to the realm of the sacred. Here, again, we are confronted

---

[23] Bartolomé de Las Casas, *The Only Way*, ed. Helen Rand Parish, trans. Francis Patrick Sullivan, Sources of American Spirituality (New York: Paulist Press, 1992), 115.

[24] This paraphrases a presentation Las Casas made at the royal court in 1542. His actual words are these: "But to be good Christians, all should feel that even though it were possible for Your Majesty to lose his entire royal dominion and for the Indians never to become Christians, if the opposite could not take place without their death and total destruction, as happened until now, it would not be unfitting for your Majesty to cease to be their lord and for them never to become Christians." See Bartolomé de Las Casas, *Bartolomé de Las Casas: A Selection of His Writings*, ed. George William Sanderlin, Borzoi Books on Latin America (New York: Knopf, 1971), 180–81.

with the issue of God and the gods, though in a crucially different form.

What could the missionaries have done instead? They could have been led by the precedent of the first four centuries, when as a minority religion Christianity confronted the so-called pagan world. The theological basis of mission in those early centuries was that the Spirit of the true God had already made himself manifest in the moral and spiritual accomplishments of pagan cultures. There was an equally strong insistence on the fact that Christ, the Second Person of the Trinity, was the seminal Logos that impregnated the whole of creation with reason, order, and truth in such a way that pagans at their best were responding to that Logos, although unaware. In other words, the best of "paganism" was a preparation for the gospel.

How different would have been the outcome if the missionaries had followed this magnificent theological precedent! Instead, out of love for the Indians and to bring them closer to the possibility of salvation, they thoroughly destroyed their whole sacred world, and held them to a standard of Christian orthodoxy in faith and practice that had no resonance in their souls. There is something impressive, even moving, in the scenes of thousands of Indians gathered in some village square or in an open field seeking the saving power of the Christian God as they professed faith in Christ and knelt to be baptized. Incidentally, the Franciscans in Mexico in twelve years, between 1524 and 1536, claim to have baptized about 5 million Indians. The Dominicans were not far behind, nor the Augustinians.[25] Of course, it is too easy to dismiss this practice as tragically naive and superficial. But these

---

25 Robert Ricard, *La Conquista Espiritual de Mexico*, trans. Ángel María Garibay K. (Mexico City: Fondo de Cultura Económica, 1947), 198–99.

compassionate missionaries were convinced there was no other way to bring the Indians to everlasting life. We must not forget that in the 16th century, and until rather recently, Catholics and Protestants held one could not be saved without a public declaration of faith in Jesus Christ.

Still, when the Indians were deprived of their whole sacred symbology, they were left bereft of the most essential sources of the self. When that happened, their validation as full human beings was no longer inherent but conditional, subject to their conformity to Christian belief and practice. In other words, any real or perceived deviancy from those norms meant a loss of rights. And we know that when people are deemed less than something, less than some standard, they are also deemed to deserve less: whether it is less food, less protection, less dignity, or, inevitably, less life. That is exactly what began to happen when Columbus seized the first six slaves on the very day of his arrival, when the missionaries destroyed the Indian realm of the sacred, and what happens now whenever a group, a color, a gender, a culture, or a religion is judged to be less.

VII. The Issue Is Idolatry

I hope that in recalling the broad contours of these 500 years from a religious and theological perspective, we have been impressed by how starkly this history raises not just questions about humanity and inhumanity, but questions also about God and the gods. Therefore, I think it is fair to raise the question, "Can we believe in God after this?" It seems to me, however, that we must hesitate before offering an orthodox response. We owe that hesitation to the millions who died before their time as a result of a colonial policy legitimized in the name of the Christian God. We owe it also to the millions in our own time that are dying as result of a policy in some way legitimized in the name of the same God or another divinity.

I guess we could as Christians begin to say that we cannot believe in the God whose name was used to cause so much suffering and death. That might indeed be an orthodox response, but it might be a bit too hasty.

We need first to ask if the god of the European abusers could perhaps be the very same god whom our churches preach and in whom we trust? Could this be the same god who blesses success and power? Could this be the same god who blessed the founding of a nation in which constitutional equality was denied blacks, Indians, and women? Could this be the same god of Manifest Destiny that sent soldiers on holy missions to subdue Mexico, the Philippines, Cuba, Puerto Rico, Nicaragua, Granada, Panama, and Iraq? Could this be the same god that for so many years made it OK to kill communists, and their wives and children? Could this be the god that has been accompanying American Protestant missionaries to convert Latin American Roman Catholics to the American Way of faith? Could this be the same god to whom we pray and whom we praise without hearing from him any command to serve the widow, the orphan, and the poor? Could this be the same god who is only accessible to us in male representation? Could this be the same god of presidential breakfasts and pious patriotic orgies? If it is not the same god of the European conquerors, the resemblance is striking.

Perhaps a realistic reading of these 500 years might help us not to believe in this god who favors the few at the expense of the many. That would be gain. But the true gain might be to regain the image of the true God. That God has been made manifest in the history of Jesus. In him, the God of the abused has become flesh to save both abused and abusers. To say this is to say that the defining issue for Christian theology is not atheism, or agnosticism, or lack of meaning, but idolatry, the struggle between God and the gods.

This is not just a restatement of orthodoxy. It is the indispensable point of departure to face head-on the question posed by the killing of the millions in places like Hispaniola, Cuba, Puerto Rico, Mexico, Peru, and more recently in Auschwitz and Treblinka, Hiroshima and Nagasaki, and in Kampuchea, Soweto, Somalia, and Sarajevo. Can one believe in God after these horrors?

I think we as Christians can respond in the affirmative only if by the revelation of Jesus Christ we are persuaded that God has been crucified as many times as innocent people have died before their time. This is not to play with words. This is not figurative language. It is the utterly realistic language of Las Casas, who sees in the suffering and dying of the Indians Jesus Christ himself, "our God, scourged, afflicted, slapped and crucified, not once, but thousands of times."[26] I think we must be prepared to believe that in some mysterious way God has taken on every unjust death, has experienced that death, with agony and screams reverberating from here to eternity in the infinity of God's self. Thank God this is a wounded God, not almighty in power, but almighty in love. And because love never dies, death will be conquered, resurrection will happen. It is happening now.

That is the only good news that overcomes the bad news of the past and that redeems history.

---

26 Gutiérrez, *Dios o el oro de las Indias*, 169.

Appendix B

Óscar Romero: Beatitude Made Flesh
*A homily given by Jorge Lara-Braud at the Austin
Presbyterian Theological Seminary
October 13, 1992*

Matthew 5:1–12

Last night I gave a lecture here at the seminary on the legacy of Columbus. I entitled it "1492–1992: Can We Believe in God after This?" It was my way of retelling the story of colonization and evangelization in the Americas from the perspective of two clashing understandings of God: the god of the abusers and the God of the abused. The abusers claimed to be acting in the name of the Christian God. That is how they protected themselves from all accountability. Not surprisingly, they sowed untold destruction. Within a century and a half after their arrival in the New World, they had caused the death of at least 49 million

Indians. It is not, therefore, flip or irreverent to ask whether we can believe in God after this.

I remain convinced that the only way for a Christian to believe in God in the light of that horror and so many others is to enter again and again into the mystery of the crucified God, the God of the abused, who takes upon himself every unjust death, letting the pain and the screams reverberate infinitely in his own self and who, out of the healing power of his love, turns every death into resurrection.

It is that motif of unjust death and awesome resurrection that is paramount in the life of Óscar Romero. I call that life "beatitude made flesh." Let me take advantage of my native language, Spanish (the language of God and the angels), to get into the meaning of beatitude. In Spanish the word is translated *bienaventuranza*—literally, good adventure to you. Like any genuine adventure, it is the confident taking of risk, the courage to defy the odds, the refusal to play it safe.

Listen, then, to how the beatitudes sound if we adopt this rendering and we paraphrase a bit:

> Good adventure to you whose hearts are genuinely with the poor: you are under God's protective rule.
>
> Good adventure to you who are without power: the whole world shall be yours;
>
> Good adventure to you who are hungry and thirsty for justice: your cup will be filled.
>
> Good adventure to you who look for truth with singleness of heart: you shall see God.
>
> Good adventure to you who work for peace: you shall be called children of God.

Good adventure to you who are persecuted for the sake of justice. You, too, are already under God's protective rule; rejoice, be very happy, when others say evil things about you falsely for my sake.

Great is your reward where God dwells.

Don't be surprised, prophets have always been an endangered species.

The original listeners were greatly taken with the poetry, but being realists, they turned down the invitation to that kind of life. The risks were too great. We who know from the record what happened to Jesus for following his own advice, could not blame them. Could we?

When you think of it, there have been relatively few who have accepted Jesus's invitation to a life of beatitude. Those who have, have kept alive for us hope in the human prospect and, more importantly, faith in the God of life.

Óscar Romero is one of those few, and for good reason we regard him as possibly the most influential saint of modern Christian history.

Let me recall highlights of his good adventure taken from the last weeks of his life.

A little over a month before his assassination, on February 17, 1980, he wrote to President Carter pleading with him that there not be any resumption of United States military aid to the government of El Salvador. The key line was this: "Please do not send weapons; they will be used for more repression against my people." As we know, the plea went unheeded. Within three years of steady escalation, El Salvador became and remained until recently the third-largest recipient of U.S. military aid in the world. The slaughter that came with it is a horror worse than anything Óscar Romero could have ever imagined. When peace finally came early this year, more than 75,000 Salvadorans had lost their lives, the vast majority noncombatants killed by the army and its paramilitary groups.

Five weeks after that letter, on Sunday, March 23, in what was to be his last radio homily, he directed another plea, this time to the soldiers:

> Do not obey your superiors when they order you to kill. You are killing your brothers and sisters. In the name of God, in the name of these suffering people whose laments rise to heaven, each day more tumultuous, I beg of you, I ask of you, I order you, in the name of God, stop the repression!

The Christian faithful in the cathedral cheered. The Christian generals were incensed. Immediately, they denounced him as a traitor in the service of international communism.

The next day, Monday, March 24, he officiated at what was to be the last Mass of his life. It was a memorial for Doña Sarita Pinto, the mother of a journalist friend.

In spite of persistent threats on his life, he allowed the Mass to be announced in the newspapers. It was held in the chapel of the cancer hospital run by the Mexican Sisters of Divine Providence.

He took for his text the familiar passage from the twelfth chapter of John used so frequently at funerals and memorial services, the passage that talks about the grain of wheat which must die to bear fruit. It was very appropriate for this occasion. Doña Sarita had given of herself generously, blessing everyone whom she touched. The parallel with the life of Jesus was obvious. So

Archbishop Romero urged everyone to follow her example, and pointing to the bread and the cup, he concluded with a reflection on the Eucharist.

"We receive here," he said, "the body of the Lord who offered himself for the redemption of the world. May his body and blood given for us nourish us in such a way that we, too, may give our body and blood like Christ, to bring justice and peace to our people. That is what Doña Sarita did. Let us, then, join ourselves to her in prayer, in the same hope and faith by which she lived."

At that moment the assassin's shot rang out!

Archbishop Romero had been standing behind the altar, facing the people. He collapsed at the foot of a large crucifix behind him. The congregants were stunned, crouching in the pews. Several women ran to him, defying the possibility of more bullets. They turned him over on his back. Blood was pouring from his mouth and nose, while he mumbled words of forgiveness.

The bullet had entered close to his heart. His vestments were turning into a sea of red, as friends frantically carried him outside to a panel truck that would take him to the nearest hospital. In the emergency room a nurse probed for a vein to start a transfusion. But the veins had collapsed. In despair, she cried out, "Oh no, his body is broken. His blood is drained. There is no more left!"

Óscar Romero died in her arms. The gentle pastor, the fearless prophet, the preacher of beatitude was no more. Through the tears, his friends began to ask, "How could he die now when we needed him the most?" "If he was not spared, is there hope for any of us who believed in him and his cause?"

The news came to me in Washington, D.C., a few hours before I was to testify to a committee of the House of Representatives against the resumption of U.S. military aid to El Salvador. After the initial shock, I began to find consolation in the memory of my last visit to him a few weeks before.

I had asked him then why he kept on taking so many risks. He told me he had no appetite for martyrdom, and that he had never been as much in love with life as he was then. His three years as archbishop of San Salvador had marked the greatest spiritual revival of the nation. The Christian poor he served had never been more alive with hope and courage, in spite of all the brutality thrown at them by the government and the death squads. What counts, he said to me, is not the length of one's years, but what we do with them. Only a life of love lives on beyond our death, he added. He concluded by quoting to me unashamedly the words of Jesus: "Greater love has no one than to lay down life for one's friends."

I carry that memory with me in the absolute conviction that Óscar Romero lived to the fullest the "good adventure" Jesus talked about, and because he did, thousands of his friends claim that death could not hold him. He is not remembered by sorrowful refrains, but by that cheerful one we hear in barrios and churches throughout the Americas: "Óscar Romero, *¡presente!*" "Óscar Romero, *¡presente!*" as the many join him in the good adventure by defending the poor, comforting the mourning, walking with the meek, and securing justice for those to whom it is denied.

God knows, it is still a risk to be merciful, to keep one's heart pure, and to make peace with one's enemies. But the much greater risk is to confuse privilege, acclaim, and self-protection with the good life.

Dear friends, it is never too early or too late to choose the life of beatitude. Should you choose to live that way, I tell you on the authority of Jesus of Nazareth and his friend Óscar Romero it will be the beginning of a good adventure that no temptation, no disappointment, not even death can take away from you.

Why not try it?

GOOD ADVENTURE TO YOU!

Notes

Unless otherwise noted, all photos are from Jorge's own personal files, albums, and archives. This is particularly important in the Oscar Romero chapter where many of the photographs may be by famous photographers of the day who followed the archbishop, but the photographer remains unknown to the author because they were just in Jorge's photo album. And while they have never before been published to my knowledge, there are similar, but not exact, photos taken at the same time period.

Foreword
1 Jorge Lara-Braud, "1492–1992: Can We Believe in God after This?" speech, Austin Presbyterian Theological Seminary, Austin, Tex., October 12, 1992 (Columbus Day); see Appendix A.
2 Ibid.
3 Jorge Lara-Braud, "Óscar Romero: Beatitude Made Flesh," homily, Austin Presbyterian Theological Seminary, Austin, Tex., October 13, 1992; see Appendix B.
4 Ibid.

On the Meaning of "Bienaventuranza"

5 James R. Brockman, Romero: A Life: The Essential Biography of a Modern Martyr and Christian Hero (Maryknoll, N.Y.: Orbis Books, 2005), 242.

Chapter 1

1. Gretchen Lara-Shartle, diary, conversation with Jorge Lara-Braud in Mexico City, May 2005.
2. Gretchen Lara-Shartle, diary, conversation with Jorge Lara-Braud and María de Jesús Lara de Espino (Cachuy, Jorge's sister) in Mexico City, May 5, 2005.
3. Although the Mexican Revolution ended in 1920, its effects were felt for years after.
4. Henry Bamford Parkes, *A History of Mexico* (Boston: Houghton Mifflin, 1969), 395.
5. Ibid., 105.
6. Joella Werlin, "Mi Jornada" (edited transcript of interviews with Jorge Lara-Braud, November 16–20, 2004), 1.

Chapter 2

7. María de Jesús de Espino, telephone interview by author, 2012.
8. Werlin, "Mi Jornada," 1–2.
9. Parkes, *History of Mexico*, 385.
10. Werlin, "Mi Jornada," 21.
11. Ibid., 3. From a footnote in "Mi Jornada": "This was 'From the Apennines to the Andes' by the mid-nineteenth-century Italian writer Edmund de Amicis, recounting the perilous journey of a very young southern Italian boy in his determined search for his mother, who had gone ahead as an immigrant to Argentina."
12. Ibid., 8.
13. Ibid.
14. Ibid.
15. Ibid.
16. Ibid., 11.

Chapter 3

17. Werlin, "Mi Jornada," 5.
18. Ibid., 6.
19. Ibid., 13.
20. Guillermo Rodriguez Braud (Jorge Lara-Braud's cousin), telephone interview by author, 2013.
21. Werlin, "Mi Jornada," 6.

Chapter 4

Epigraph—Martin Luther King Jr. and Clayborne Carson, *The Autobiography of Martin Luther King, Jr.* (London: Abacus, 2006). 755–56.

22. Werlin, "Mi Jornada," 15.
23. Ibid.
24. Ibid.

NOTES

25 Ibid., 14.
26 Ibid., 15–16.
27 Ibid., 16.

Chapter 5

28 Jorge Lara-Braud, "Has It Been Worth It? Yes, It Really Has," speech, First United Methodist Church, Austin, Tex., July 8, 1997.
29 All photographs of Mr. and Mrs. Cobbs and the Tex-Mex Building provided by their granddaughter, Karen McCulloch.
30 Ibid.
31 Werlin, "Mi Jornada," 21.
32 Lara-Braud, "Has It Been Worth It?"
33 Ibid.
34 Ibid.

Chapter 6

35 Date and photographer unknown, from *254 Texas Courthouses* website, accessed July 20, 2022, http://www.254texascourthouses.net/122-kleberg-county.html.
36 Acts 16:28–34 NRSV.
37 William R. Jarvis, recreational director, photograph, 1954, *Presbyterian Pan American School Records*, A2016-017.0653, South Texas Archives, James C. Jernigan Library, Texas A&M University–Kingsville.
38 Werlin, "Mi Jornada," 26–27. The entire story of Jorge's experience and the dialogue in Wharton, Texas, is from "Mi Jornada."

Chapter 7

39 Dave Faries, "Days Gone Bite: Frito Bandito," *Dallas Observer*, January 27, 2010, http://www.dallasobserver.com/restaurants/days-gone-bite-frito-bandito-7029410. The Frito Bandito was a racially controversial mascot for Fritos® corn chips in the late 1960s and early 1970s.
40 Werlin, "Mi Jornada," 28–29.
41 Ibid.
42 Ibid., 23.
43 *Chromascope '54*, editor Carolyn Hall, Austin College yearbook.
44 Werlin, "Mi Jornada," 51–52.
45 Ibid., 52.
46 David Detzer, *The Brink: Cuban Missile Crisis, 1962* (New York: Thomas Y. Crowell, 1979), 17.
47 Werlin, "Mi Jornada," 51–52.
48 Arthur M. Schlesinger, *The Dynamics of World Power: A Documentary History of United States Foreign Policy, 1945–1973* (New York: McGraw-Hill, 1973), 521.
49 Genie Hopper, telephone interview by author, March 2012. At the time of the Mexico City visit, Hopper was director of Christian education at Austin Presbyterian Theological Seminary.
50 Werlin, "Mi Jornada," 30–31.

51 Stephanie A. Mann, "The Mexican Government versus the Catholic Church," *Catholic Exchange*, April 9, 2012, http://catholicexchange.com/the-mexican-government-versus-the-catholic-church.
52 Werlin, "Mi Jornada," 32.
53 Ibid., 31.
54 It may seem strange to people in the United States that even people in the same family would refer to others by their formal name. As a sign of respect, Cachuy and I always referred to him as Señor Marroquín. The children in the family called him "Papágrande." People outside the family referred to him as Don Hazael.

Chapter 8

55 Luke 3:22 NRSV.
56 Jorge Lara-Braud to Very Dear Friends, August 12, 1962, Mexico City.
57 Werlin, "Mi Jornada," 37.
58 Jeanne Williams, "New Institute Established as Research Training Center," *Texas Presbyterian* 5, no. 12 (December 1965): 1, 6.
59 John Calvin, "Scandal in the Church No Occasion for Leaving It," in *Institutes of the Christian Religion*, vol. 2, bk 4 (Louisville: Westminster John Knox Press, 1960), 1026–28.
60 Werlin, "Mi Jornada," 34.
61 Jorge Lara-Braud, "No Longer Strangers: The Week of Prayer for Christian Unity," speech (unknown location), October 3, 1977.
62 Alberto Rosales Pérez, *Historia de la Iglesia Nacional Presbiteriana El Divino Salvador, 1889–1922*, (Mexico City: Casa de Publicaciones El Faro, 1998), 46.
63 Jorge Lara-Braud to Gretchen Lara-Shartle, May 9, 1983, Atlanta, Ga.
64 Werlin, "Mi Jornada," 33–34.
65 Matthew 27:11 NRSV.
66 Werlin, "Mi Jornada," 34.
67 Ibid.
68 Lara-Braud, "Has It Been Worth It?"
69 Werlin, "Mi Jornada," 34. The account of this whole faculty-student meeting is from "Mi Jornada."
70 Ibid.
71 Salatiel Palomino, telephone interview by author, November 2011.
72 Werlin, "Mi Jornada," 35.
73 Ibid.
74 The quotation from Jorge regarding Vatican II and Pope John XXIII comes from a handout that Jorge produced for a class he taught on liberation theology at San Francisco Theological Seminary in 1988.

Chapter 9

75 C. H. Hwang, "Come, Creator Spirit! For the Calling of the Churches Together," *Ecumenical Review* 16, no. 5 (October 1964): 484–99.
76 Jorge Lara-Braud, "The Hispanic-American Institute: A Retrospective," address, Presbyterian Ministry of Texas: History's Lessons for Tomorrow's Mission,

NOTES

symposium sponsored by Presbyterian Historical Society of the Southwest, Austin Presbyterian Theological Seminary, Austin, Tex., March 9, 1996, 5.

77 "We hold these truths to be self-evident, that all men are created equal, that they are endowed by their Creator with certain unalienable Rights, that among these are Life, Liberty and the pursuit of Happiness." Declaration of Independence.

78 Jorge Lara-Braud, "At Home in the New Creation," address, Summer Commencement, Austin College, Sherman, Tex., August 25, 1967, 9.

79 "What Is La Raza Unida?" *Texas Presbyterian* 8, no. 4 (April 1968): 6.

80 Jorge Lara-Braud, "Mission in Partnership," address, Montreat World Mission Conference, Montreat, N.C., July 29, 1963, 9.

81 Jorge Lara-Braud, "By Means of the Cross He United Both Races: Reflections on Inter-Ethnic Conflict and Reconciliation Where the Cultures of the Americas Meet in the U.S.A.," *Austin Seminary Bulletin (Faculty Edition)* 83, no. 7 (April 1968): 42–46.

82 Ibid.

83 "What Is La Raza Unida?," 6.

84 Jorge Lara-Braud to John Mackay, March 15, 1968, Hispanic-American Institute records, accession no. 1996-079, Austin Seminary Archives, Stitt Library, Austin Presbyterian Theological Seminary, Austin, Tex.

85 Sherwood H. Reisner letter to Jorge Lara-Braud, April 27, 1968, Hispanic-American Institute records, accession no. 1996-079, Austin Seminary Archives, Stitt Library, Austin Presbyterian Theological Seminary, Austin, Tex.

86 James S. Currie, *Planting Trees: A History of Presbyterian Pan American School* (Waco: Nortex Press, 2011), 108.

87 Helen Parmley, "Don't Invite Prof as 'Ethnic Speaker,'" *Dallas Morning News*, August 22, 1970.

88 PADRES was a national association of priests. The acronym stands for the Spanish *Padres Asociados para Derechos Religiosos, Educativos, y Sociales*, which translates as Priests Associated for Religious, Educational, and Social Rights.

89 Werlin, "Mi Jornada," 41–42.

Chapter 10

90 Jorge Luis Lara-Marroquín, telephone interview by author, February 2012.

91 Ibid.

92 Ibid.

93 Ibid.

94 Ibid.

95 The author lacks materials such as journals or interviews to include more about Jorge's second and third marriages.

96 According to its website, the National Council of Churches "partners with secular and interfaith partners to advance a shared agenda of peace, progress, and positive change." See https://nationalcouncilofchurches.us/about-us/.

97 Jorge Lara-Braud, "Celebrating Our Diversities," speech, General Assembly of The Christian Church, Disciples of Christ, San Antonio, Tex., August 16, 1975.

98 Photo by *National Catholic Reporter* from Jorge's personal files. Reprinted by permission of NCR Publishing Company www.NCROnline.org.

Chapter 11

99 Epigraph—"Central America: A Season of Martyrs," special issue of *Christianity and Crisis*, May 12, 1980, front cover. Jorge Lara-Braud, "Óscar Romero: They Killed Him for Telling the Truth, and He Rose Again in the El Salvadoran People," speech, commemorating the 20th anniversary of the martyrdom of Óscar Arnulfo Romero, Metropolitan Cathedral of San Salvador, El Salvador, March 21, 2000.

100 Richard A. Haggerty, *El Salvador: A Country Study*, Area Handbook Series (Washington, D.C.: U.S. Government Printing Office, Secretary of the Army, 1990), https://archive.org/details/elsalvadorcountr00hagg.

101 *Encyclopaedia Britannica*, s.v. "El Salvador: Military Dictatorships," https://www.britannica.com/place/El-Salvador/Military-dictatorships#ref468011.

102 Image from the MUPI Collection (Museo de la Palabra y la Imagen), photographer and title unknown, accessed January 19, 2022, https://www.elsalvadorperspectives.com/2018/10/carlos-calleja-and-arenas-past.html.

103 Brockman, *Romero: A Life*, 34–35.

104 Ibid., 36.

105 Ibid., 38.

106 Ibid., 47.

107 Image from the CAFOD website (Catholic Agency for Oversees Development), date, photographer, and title unknown, accessed January 19, 2022, https://cafod.org.uk/News/International-news/Oscar-Romero-life-timeline.

108 Michael E. Lee, "Archbishop Oscar Romero Was Gunned Down inside His Own Church 38 Years Ago: Soon He'll Become El Salvador's First Saint," *The Conversation*, March 23, 2018, https://theconversation.com/archbishop-oscar-romero-was-gunned-down-inside-his-own-church-38-years-ago-soon-hell-become-el-salvadors-first-saint-93331.

109 Brockman, *Romero: A Life*, 5.

110 Jorge Lara-Braud, 1979, Notes on El Salvador, handwritten spiral notebook from various trips Jorge made to El Salvador.

111 Alan Riding, "Salvadoran Vote Unrest Raises Fear of Polarization," *The New York Times*, March 20, 1977, Late City Edition, 13, https://www.nytimes.com/1977/03/20/archives/salvadoran-vote-unrest-raises-fear-of-polarization.html.

112 Lara-Braud, Notes on El Salvador.

113 Lara-Braud, "Óscar Romero: They Killed Him for Telling the Truth."

114 Date, photographer, and title unknown, Santa Clara University Ignatian Center for Jesuit Education, accessed January 19, 2022, https://www.scu.edu/ic/media--publications/articles/article-stories/a-life-of-faith-and-courage.html.

115 Lara-Braud, Notes on El Salvador.

116 Photographer and title unknown, March 1977, El Salvador, https://www.peoplesworld.org/article/remembering-father-rutilio-grande-of-el-salvador/.

117 Lara-Braud, "Óscar Romero: They Killed Him for Telling the Truth."

118 Lara-Braud, Notes on El Salvador.

119 Raymond Bonner, *Weakness and Deceit: America and El Salvador's Dirty War* (New York: OR Books, 2016).

120 Lara-Braud, "Óscar Romero: They Killed Him for Telling the Truth."

NOTES

121 Photo from Jorge's personal files; date, photographer, and location unknown.
122 Lara-Braud, "Óscar Romero: They Killed Him for Telling the Truth."
123 Lara-Braud, "Has It Been Worth It?"
124 Jorge Lara-Braud, "An Assassination that Speaks to Us of Resurrection, Third Sunday in Ordinary Time Funeral Mass for Fr Octavio Ortiz Luna, The Archbishop Romero Trust, January 21, 1979, http://www.romerotrust.org.uk/homilies-and-writings/homilies/assassination-speaks-us-resurrection.
125 Lara-Braud, Notes on El Salvador.
126 Ibid.
127 Jorge Lara-Braud, "Love Your Enemy as Yourself," homily, El Buen Pastor Presbyterian Church, Austin, Tex., February 19, 1995.
128 Werlin, "Mi Jornada," 45–46. The entire story and the dialogue with the base ecclesial community comes from "Mi Jornada."
129 Location and date are based on a well-known photograph taken by Octavio Duran for the Catholic News Service, though it is not certain if Duran took this photo as well. The photo is from Jorge's personal photo album with no notations, and the Duran photo is also in his album in black-and-white. The woman beside Jorge is seen in the Duran photo as well, which can be viewed at https://www.catholicsun.org/2020/03/23/in-the-40-years-since-st-oscar-romeros-death-many-things-have-shifted/.
130 Lara-Braud, "Has It Been Worth It?"
131 Óscar Arnulfo Romero, *Voice of the Voiceless: The Four Pastoral Letters and Other Statements*, ed. William E. Jerman (Maryknoll, N.Y.: Orbis Books, 1985), 181–82.
132 Photographer unknown, February 2, 1980, Louvain, Belguim, KU Levun, accessed April 5, 2022, https://www.kuleuven.be/english/romero.
133 Romero, *Voice of the Voiceless*, 181–82.
134 Lara-Braud, Appendix B.
135 Photo by Etienne Montes, in Carolyn Forché, *El Salvador: Work of Thirty Photographers*, ed. Harry Mattison, Susan Meiselas, and Fae Rubenstein (New York: Writers and Readers, 1983), 29.
136 Photo by Chris Steele-Perkins/Magnum, in Forché, *El Salvador: Work of Thirty Photographers*, 60.
137 Lara-Braud, Appendix B.
138 Photo from Jorge's personal files; date, photographer, and location unknown. Jorge also spoke at this event.
139 Brockman, *Romero: A Life*, 244.
140 Lara-Braud, Appendix B.
141 Alma Guillermoprieto, "Death Comes for the Archbishop," *New York Review*, May 27, 2010, http://www.nybooks.com/articles/2010/05/27/death-comes-archbishop/.
142 Lara-Braud, Appendix B.
143 Photo by Eulalio Pérez, March 24, 1980, in the chapel of Hospital of Divine Providence, San Salvador, https://elfaro.net/en/202003/el_salvador/24088/A-5-Millimeter-Hole.htm.
144 Lara-Braud, Appendix B. The principal source for these final moments in the archbishop's life is the homily "Óscar Romero: Beatitude Made Flesh."

145 Photographer and title unknown, Associated Press file photo, March 24, 1980, Hospital of Divine Providence, San Salvador. Accessed February 8, 2022, https://cuslar.org/2015/03/23/35th-anniversary-of-oscar-romeros-assassination-a-lenten-reflection/.
146 Lara-Braud, "Has It Been Worth It?" The dialogue and story of the nuns comes directly from the speech.
147 Werlin, "Mi Jornada," 49.
148 Lara-Braud, "Has It Been Worth It?" Leah Wilson and Alexis Stoumbelis, "'Removing the Veil': El Salvador Apologizes for State Violence on 20th Anniversary of Peace Accords," The North American Congress on Latin America, https://nacla.org/news/2012/1/17/%E2%80%98removing-veil%E2%80%99-el-salvador-apologizes-state-violence-20th-anniversary-peace-accords.
149 Photo by Eugene Richards/Magnum, in Forché, *El Salvador: Work of Thirty Photographers*, 89.
150 Reverend Bill Wipfler, telephone interview by author, September 2012.
151 Photo by Etienne Montes, March 30, 1980, in Forché, *El Salvador: Work of Thirty Photographers*, 33.
152 Photo by Etienne Montes, March 30, 1980, in Forché, *El Salvador: Work of Thirty Photographers*, 34.
153 Associated Press, "UPITN 3 4 80 Violence Breaks Out at The Funeral Service or Archbishop Oscar Romero," YouTube video, June 5, 2018, https://www.youtube.com/watch?v=k4MscBN9UxQ&t=10s (still is taken at the 0:52 mark).
154 Jorge Lara-Braud, "El Pueblo Unido Jamas Sera Vencido," in "Central America: A Season of Martyrs," special issue of *Christianity and Crisis* 40, no. 8 (May 12, 1980): 114, 148–50.
155 Photo by Etienne Montes, March 30, 1980, in Forché, *El Salvador: Work of Thirty Photographers*, 34.
156 Lara-Braud, "El Pueblo Unido Jamas Sera Vencido."
157 Ibid.
158 Ibid., 149. While the actual document that the dignitaries signed is not contained in the article Jorge wrote for *Christianity and Crisis*, he does give a synopsis of how the group met, collaborated, and even spoke with the "leftists" whom the government blamed for the massacre. The leftist account concurred with the account of the dignitaries. The actual document can be found on the Archbishop Romero Trust website, http://www.romerotrust.org.uk/gallery/Romero%20Funeral.
159 Lara-Braud, Appendix B.

Chapter 12

160 Lara-Braud, "Óscar Romero: They Killed Him for Telling the Truth." Epigraph—Gretchen Lara-Shartle, *Awakening Courage: One Woman's Journey* (Austin, Tex.: Good Adventure Press, 2022), 124.
161 "A Brief Explanation by Jorge Lara-Braud Concerning the Paper 'Christians and Jews: A Unique Relationship,'" Jorge Lara-Braud, March 4, 2000, Austin, Tex.
162 Jorge to Gretchen, May 9, 1983.
163 Gretchen Lara-Shartle, diary, April 17–19, 1983.

NOTES

164 Lara-Shartle, *Awakening Courage*, 83.
165 Date, photographer, and location unknown, from *On This Deity*, accessed July 13, 2022, https://www.onthisdeity.com/21st-february-1934-%E2%80%93-the-death-of-augusto-cesar-sandino/.
166 Washingtonmonthly.com, accessed November 22, 2019, https://washingtonmonthly.com/2006/05/16/but-hes-our-son-of-a-bitch/.
167 Clifford L. Staten, *The History of Nicaragua* (Santa Barbara, Calif.: Greenwood Press, 2010), 77.
168 Ibid., 77–78.
169 Ibid., 86.
170 Walter Lafeber, *Inevitable Revolutions: The United States in Central America*, 2nd ed. (New York: W. W. Norton, 1993), 235.
171 Staten, *History of Nicaragua*, 86.
172 Lafeber, *Inevitable Revolutions*, 238.
173 From Chuck Gomez, "The Virginia Shooting Reminds Me of a Colleague's Execution 36 Years Ago," August 31, 2015, https://www.huffpost.com/entry/reality-murder-videotapin_b_8052042 (Courtesy www.LiveLeak.com).
174 Matthew C. Dallette and Mary E. Pritchard, letter to the editor, "Nicaragua Paying Somoza's U.S. Debt," *New York Times*, June 30, 1985.
175 Thomas W. Walker and Christine J. Wade, *Nicaragua: Living in the Shadow of the Eagle*, 5th ed. (Boulder, Colo.: Westview Press, 2011), 158–59.
176 Luis Enrique Mejía Godoy, "Revenge: Using the Words of the Sandinista Freedom Fighter, Tomás Borge," translated from the Spanish by Dinah Livingstone, *New Internationalist*, May 1, 2007, https://newint.org/features/2007/05/01/poem.
177 Walker and Wade, *Nicaragua*, 46.
178 Dr. Ulrike Hanemann, *Nicaragua's Literacy Campaign*, report no. 2006/ED/EFA/MRT/PI/43, UNESCO Institute for Education, March 2006, https://unesdoc.unesco.org/ark:/48223/pf0000146007.
179 "Understanding the Iran-Contra Affairs," https://www.brown.edu/Research/Understanding_the_Iran_Contra_Affair/n-contras.php.
180 Mejía Godoy, "Revenge."
181 Phil Davison, "Tomas Borge: Last Surviving Founder of the Sandinistas," *The Independent*, May 2, 2012, https://www.independent.co.uk/news/obituaries/tomas-borge-last-surviving-founder-of-the-sandinistas-7704217.html.
182 Lara-Shartle, diary, 1983.
183 Lara-Shartle, *Awakening Courage*, 108–9.
184 Ibid., 117. Ray Bonner (speaking of himself in the third person) gave a telephone interview to the author in July of 1997 from Vienna in which he said: "Criticism from *The Wall Street Journal* and the Reagan administration had an impact on Bonner's career. There were editors at the paper who were concerned about his reporting. Eventually, he was pulled out of Central America and put on the business beat. That was a very sensitive time. It is hard to recall so long ago. We were reliving the fifties. Everybody was afraid of being seen as soft on communism. Congress had no balls" (ibid., 118).
185 From its website (http://carecendc.org/about/history/): "The Central American Resource Center (CARECEN), originally named the Central

American Refugee Center, was established in 1981 and incorporated in 1982 to meet the needs of refugees fleeing a period of violence and strife in Central America. El Salvador, Nicaragua and Guatemala all experienced civil wars during the 1980s and 1990s, and Honduras suffered more than a decade of civil strife in the form of a 'dirty war.' Many Central Americans, seeking refuge from the violence in their home countries, fled to neighboring nations including Mexico and the United States."

186 Lara-Shartle, *Awakening Courage*, 126.

Chapter 13

187 Jorge Lara-Braud to Gretchen Lara-Shartle, December 5, 1983, Atlanta, Ga.
188 Jorge Lara-Braud to Gretchen Lara-Shartle, July 15, 1983, Atlanta, Ga.
189 *Ebenezer* literally means "stone of help." It is taken directly from Samuel 7:7–12 and refers to the site where Samuel erected a memorial stone marking the place where the Philistines were finally vanquished by the Israelites.
190 Lara-Braud to Lara-Shartle, July 15, 1983.
191 Jorge Lara-Braud to Gretchen Lara-Shartle, August 7, 1983, Atlanta, Ga.
192 Gretchen Lara-Shartle, diary, December 19, 1983.
193 Jorge Lara-Braud, Diary, March 5, 1983.
194 Lara-Braud to Lara-Shartle, August 7, 1983.
195 Ibid.
196 Lara-Shartle, *Awakening Courage*, 121.
197 Ibid.
198 "Summer 1986," Gretchen Lara-Shartle and Jorge Lara-Braud to Friends and Family, July 29, 1986, Avignon, France.
199 Gretchen Lara-Shartle to Kyria Sabin, September 21, 1986, San Anselmo, Calif.
200 Tim Lanham, telephone interview by author, May 2013.
201 María de Jesús Lara de Espino to Gretchen Lara-Shartle and Jorge Lara-Braud, August 7, 1986, Mexico City.
202 Ibid.
203 Gretchen Lara-Shartle to María de Jesús Lara de Espino, September 23, 1989, San Anselmo, Calif.
204 Tim Lanham to Gretchen Lara-Shartle and Jorge Lara-Braud, December 25, 1989, Des Moines, Iowa.
205 Lanham, telephone interview, May 2013.

Chapter 14

206 Jorge Lara-Braud to Howard and Nancy Rice, December 5, 1992, Austin, Tex.
207 Lara-Braud, Appendix A.
208 Ibid.
209 Jorge Lara-Braud to Sister Veronique, December 5, 1992, Austin, Tex.
210 Ibid.
211 Jorge Lara-Braud to Ms. Sylvia Washer, executive presbyter of Mission Presbyterian Church, and Rev. Vicki Yates, chair of Commission Presbytery, September 7, 1995, El Buen Pastor Presbyterian Church, Austin, Tex.
212 Ibid.

NOTES

213 Kevin Virobik-Adams, photographer, in article "Voices of Easter," *Austin American-Statesman*, March 30, 1997, El Buen Pastor Presbyterian Church, Austin, Tex.
214 Lara-Braud to Washer.
215 Revelation 21:4 NRSV.
216 Jorge Lara-Braud, A Meditation at the Memorial Service for Thomas Howes Shartle, First United Methodist Church, Crockett, Tex., January 21, 1997.
217 Jorge Lara-Braud to Rev. Laura Mendenhall, pastor of Westminster Presbyterian Church, December 27, 1994, Austin, Tex. The story of Doña Lencha appears almost verbatim in Jorge's letter to Reverend Mendenhall.

Chapter 15

218 Jorge Lara-Braud to Very Dear Relatives and Friends, August 16, 2000, Austin, Tex.
219 Walter Wink and June Keener Wink to Jorge Lara-Braud, September 5, 2000, Sandisfield, Mass.
220 "Clarita, mi muy querida nietecita," Jorge Lara-Braud to Clara Pollock, September 20, 2000, Mexico City.
221 "Julia," interview by Jan Williams, November 6, 2010, Austin, Tex.
222 Ida Garcia de Espino, telephone interview by author, February 12, 2011.
223 Jorge Lara-Braud, e-mail message to Gretchen Lara-Shartle (never sent), July 31, 2003.
224 Gretchen Lara-Shartle, diary, August 2003.
225 Gretchen Lara-Shartle, diary, February 26, 2003.
226 Gretchen Lara-Shartle, diary, July 23, 2003.
227 Jorge Lara-Braud dictated to Gretchen Lara-Shartle, October 7, 2003, a toast to be given by Gretchen at the wedding of Greta Sabin and Daniel Weisser on October 11, 2003, Austin, Tex.
228 Gretchen Lara-Shartle, diary, December 11, 2003.
229 Gretchen Lara-Shartle, diary, October 26, 2003.
230 Cynthia Bourgeault, *Love Is Stronger than Death: The Mystical Union of Two Souls* (New York: Bell Tower, 1999).

Afterword

231 Jalaluddin Rumi, "The Wonderful Results of Taming," in *You Are Not What You Think: The Egoless Path to Self-Esteem and Generous Love*, by David Richo (Boston: Shambhala Publications, 2015), 139.
232 Paraphrased from Mary Oliver, "When Death Comes," in *New and Selected Poems*, vol. 1 (Boston: Beacon Press, 1992), 10. The poem reads:
. . . I was a bride married to amazement.
I was the bridegroom, taking the world into my arms.
233 Judith Liro, "Sermon for Jorge Lara-Braud," El Buen Pastor Presbyterian Church, Austin, Tex., July 26, 2008.

Bibliography

Jorge's speeches, diaries, writings, and letters are unpublished and in the author's possession. Of the unpublished items noted in the text, only the speeches are listed below.

Bonner, Raymond. *Weakness and Deceit: America and El Salvador's Dirty War*. New York: OR Books, 2016.

Bourgeault, Cynthia. *Love Is Stronger than Death: The Mystical Union of Two Souls*. New York: Bell Tower, 1999.

Brockman, James R. *Romero: A Life: The Essential Biography of a Modern Martyr and Christian Hero*. Maryknoll, N.Y.: Orbis Book, 2005.

Calvin, John. "Scandal in the Church No Occasion for Leaving It." In *Institutes of the Christian Religion*, vol. 2, bk. 4. Louisville, Ky.: Westminster John Knox Press, 1960.

"Central America: A Season of Martyrs." Special issue of *Christianity and Crisis* 40, no. 8 (May 12, 1980). Front cover.

Cummins, John. *The Voyage of Christopher Columbus: Columbus' Own Journal of Discovery, Newly Restored and Translated*. London: Weidenfeld and Nicolson, 1991.

Currie, James S. *Planting Trees: A History of Presbyterian Pan American School*. Waco: Nortex Press, 2011.

Davies, Hunter. *In Search of Columbus*. London: Sinclair Stevenson. 1991.

Denevan, William M. *The Native Population of the Americas in 1492*. Madison: University of Wisconsin Press, 1976.

Detzer, David. *The Brink: Cuban Missile Crisis, 1962*. New York: Thomas Y. Crowell, 1979.

"El Salvador: Military Dictatorships." Encyclopaedia Britannica. https://www.britannica.com/place/El-Salvador/Military-dictatorships#ref468011.

Forché, Carolyn, *El Salvador: Work of Thirty Photographers*. Edited by Harry Mattison, Susan Meiselas, and Fae Rubenstein. New York: Writers and Readers, 1983.

Guillermoprieto, Alma. "Death Comes for the Archbishop." *New York Review*, May 27, 2010. http://www.nybooks.com/articles/2010/05/27/death-comes-archbishop/.

Gutiérrez, Gustavo. *Dios o el oro de las Indias*. Lima: Instituto Bartolomé de Las Casas, 1989.

Haggerty, Richard A. *El Salvador: A Country Study*. Area Handbook Series. Washington, D.C.: U.S. Government Printing Office, Secretary of the Army, 1990. https://archive.org/details/elsalvadorcountr00hagg.

Hanemann, Dr. Ulrike. *Nicaragua's Literacy Campaign*. Report no. 2006/ED/EFA/MRT/PI/43. UNESCO Institute for Education. March 2006. Background paper prepared for the Education for All Global Monitoring Report 2006 *Literacy for Life*. https://unesdoc.unesco.org/ark:/48223/pf0000146007.

Hwang, C. H. "Come, Creator Spirit! For the Calling of the Churches Together." *Ecumenical Review* 16, no. 5 (October 1964). World Council of Churches.

King, Martin Luther, Jr., and Clayborne Carson. *The Autobiography of Martin Luther King Jr*. London: Abacus, 2006.

Koning, Hans. *Columbus: His Enterprise*. New York: Monthly Review Press, 1976.

Lafeber, Walter. *Inevitable Revolutions: The United States in Central America*. 2nd ed. New York: W. W. Norton, 1993.

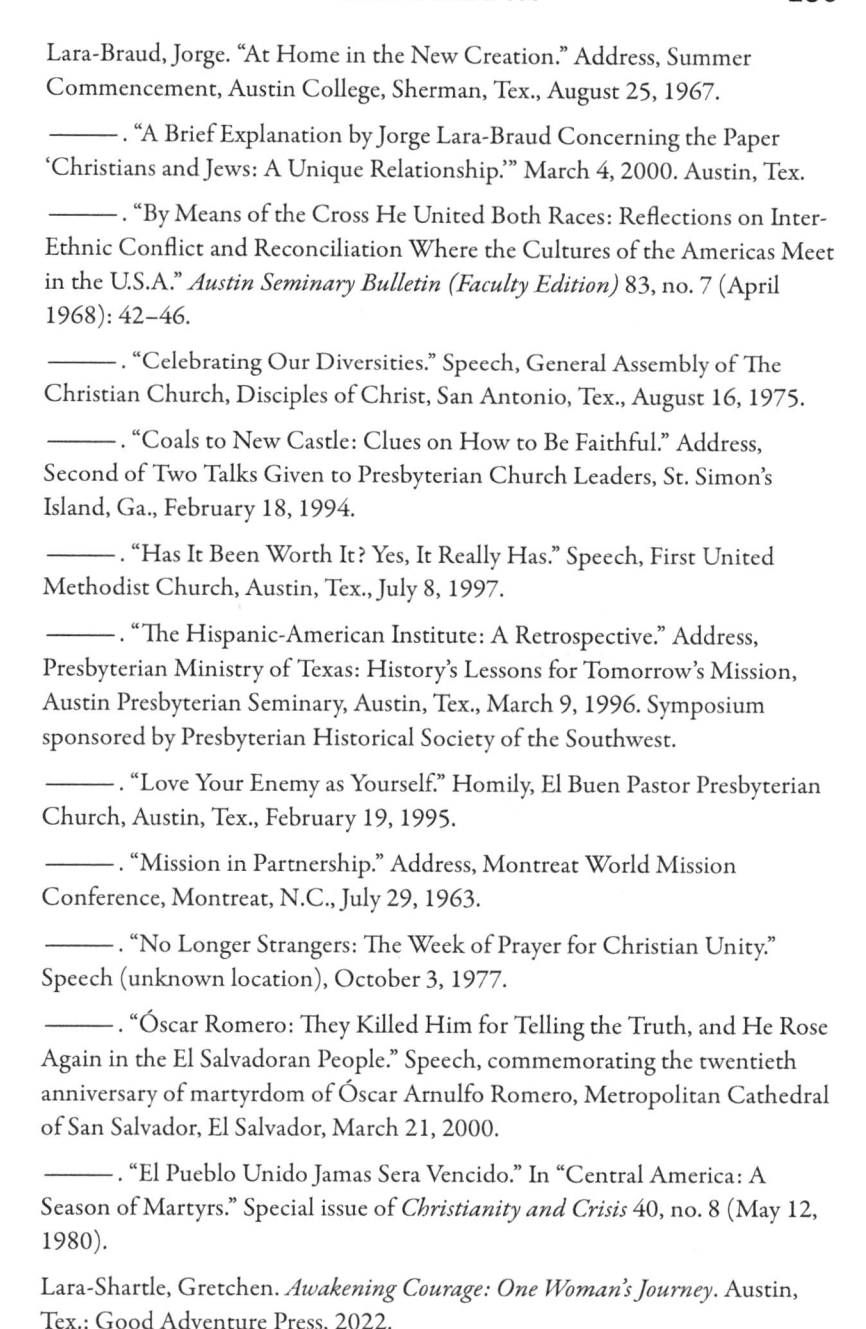

Lara-Braud, Jorge. "At Home in the New Creation." Address, Summer Commencement, Austin College, Sherman, Tex., August 25, 1967.

———. "A Brief Explanation by Jorge Lara-Braud Concerning the Paper 'Christians and Jews: A Unique Relationship.'" March 4, 2000. Austin, Tex.

———. "By Means of the Cross He United Both Races: Reflections on Inter-Ethnic Conflict and Reconciliation Where the Cultures of the Americas Meet in the U.S.A." *Austin Seminary Bulletin (Faculty Edition)* 83, no. 7 (April 1968): 42–46.

———. "Celebrating Our Diversities." Speech, General Assembly of The Christian Church, Disciples of Christ, San Antonio, Tex., August 16, 1975.

———. "Coals to New Castle: Clues on How to Be Faithful." Address, Second of Two Talks Given to Presbyterian Church Leaders, St. Simon's Island, Ga., February 18, 1994.

———. "Has It Been Worth It? Yes, It Really Has." Speech, First United Methodist Church, Austin, Tex., July 8, 1997.

———. "The Hispanic-American Institute: A Retrospective." Address, Presbyterian Ministry of Texas: History's Lessons for Tomorrow's Mission, Austin Presbyterian Seminary, Austin, Tex., March 9, 1996. Symposium sponsored by Presbyterian Historical Society of the Southwest.

———. "Love Your Enemy as Yourself." Homily, El Buen Pastor Presbyterian Church, Austin, Tex., February 19, 1995.

———. "Mission in Partnership." Address, Montreat World Mission Conference, Montreat, N.C., July 29, 1963.

———. "No Longer Strangers: The Week of Prayer for Christian Unity." Speech (unknown location), October 3, 1977.

———. "Óscar Romero: They Killed Him for Telling the Truth, and He Rose Again in the El Salvadoran People." Speech, commemorating the twentieth anniversary of martyrdom of Óscar Arnulfo Romero, Metropolitan Cathedral of San Salvador, El Salvador, March 21, 2000.

———. "El Pueblo Unido Jamas Sera Vencido." In "Central America: A Season of Martyrs." Special issue of *Christianity and Crisis* 40, no. 8 (May 12, 1980).

Lara-Shartle, Gretchen. *Awakening Courage: One Woman's Journey*. Austin, Tex.: Good Adventure Press, 2022.

Las Casas, Bartolomé de. *Bartolomé de Las Casas: A Selection of His Writings*. Edited and translated by George William Sanderlin. Borzoi Books on Latin America. New York: Knopf, 1971.

———. *Historia de Las Indias*. Vol. 1. Edited by Agustín Millares Carlo. Introduction by Lewis Hanke. Mexico City: Fondo de Cultura Económica, 1951.

———. *The Only Way*. Edited by Helen Rand Parish. Translated by Francis Patrick Sullivan. Sources of American Spirituality. New York: Paulist Press, 1992.

———. *Tratados de Fray Bartolomé de Las Casas*. Vol 2. Translated by Juan Pérez De Tudela Bueso, Agustín Millares Carlo, and Rafael Moreno. Mexico City: Fondo de Cultura Económica, 1997.

Lee, Michael E. "Archbishop Oscar Romero Was Gunned Down inside His Own Church 38 Years Ago: Soon He'll Become El Salvador's First Saint." *The Conversation*, March 23, 2018. https://theconversation.com/archbishop-oscar-romero-was-gunned-down-inside-his-own-church-38-years-ago-soon-hell-become-el-salvadors-first-saint-93331.

Liro, Judith. "Sermon for Jorge Lara-Braud." El Buen Pastor Presbyterian Church, Austin, Tex., July 25, 2008. In the author's possession.

Mann, Stephanie A. "The Mexican Government versus the Catholic Church." *Catholic Exchange*, April 9, 2012. http://catholicexchange.com/the-mexican-government-versus-the-catholic-church.

McKennie, H. *Goodpasture, Cross and Sword*. Maryknoll, N.Y.: Orbis Books, 1989.

Mejía Godoy, Luis Enrique. "Revenge: Using the Words of the Sandinista Freedom Fighter, Tomás Borge." *New Internationalist*. May 1, 2007. https://newint.org/features/2007/05/01/poem.

Morison, Samuel Eliot. *Admiral of the Ocean Sea*. 2 vols. Boston: Little, Brown, 1942.

———. *Christopher Columbus: Mariner*. New York: New American Library, 1942.

National Council for the Social Studies. "The Columbian Quincentenary: An Educational Opportunity." *History Teacher* 25, no. 2 (February 1992): 145–52.

BIBLIOGRAPHY

Oliver, Mary. "When Death Comes." In *New and Selected Poems*, vol. 1. Boston: Beacon Press, 1992.

Parkes, Henry Bamford. *A History of Mexico*. Boston: Houghton Mifflin, 1969.

Ricard, Robert. *La Conquista Espiritual de Mexico*. Translated by Ángel María Garibay K. Mexico City: Fondo de Cultura Económica, 1947.

Romero, Óscar Arnulfo. *Voice of the Voiceless: The Four Pastoral Letters and Other Statements*. Edited by William E. Jerman. Maryknoll, N.Y.: Orbis Books, 1985.

Rosales Pérez, Alberto. *Historia de la Iglesia Nacional Presbiteriana* El Divino Salvador, *1889–1922*. Mexico City: Casa de Publicaciones El Faro, 1998.

Rumi, Jalaluddin. "The Wonderful Results of Taming." In *You Are Not What You Think: The Egoless Path to Self-Esteem and Generous Love*, by David Richo. Boston: Shambhala Publications, 2015.

Schlesinger, Arthur M., Jr. *The Dynamics of World Power: A Documentary History of United States Foreign Policy, 1945–1973*. New York: McGraw-Hill, 1973.

Staten, Clifford L. *The History of Nicaragua*. Santa Barbara, Calif.: Greenwood Press, 2010.

Taviani, Paolo. *Christopher Columbus: The Grand Design*. London: Orbis Books, 1985.

"Understanding the Iran-Contra Affairs." https://www.brown.edu/Research/Understanding_the_Iran_Contra_Affair/n-contras.php.

Walker, Thomas W., and Christine J. Wade. *Nicaragua: Living in the Shadow of the Eagle*. 5th ed. Boulder, Colo.: Westview Press, 2011.

Werlin, Joella. "Mi Jornada." Edited transcript of interviews with Jorge Lara-Braud, November 16–20, 2004. In the author's possession.

Wilson, Leah, and Alexis Stoumbelis. "'Removing the Veil': El Salvador Apologizes for State Violence on 20th Anniversary of Peace Accords." The North American Congress on Latin America. https://nacla.org/news/2012/1/17/%E2%80%98removing-veil%E2%80%99-el-salvador-apologizes-state-violence-20th-anniversary-peace-accords.

Yewell, John, and Chris Dodge. *Confronting Columbus: An Anthology*. Jefferson, N.C.: McFarland & Company, 1992.